Worship *and* Eucharist

Worship *and* Eucharist

The Whole Christ, Head and Body

DOUGLAS H. KNIGHT

CASCADE *Books* • Eugene, Oregon

WORSHIP AND EUCHARIST
The Whole Christ, Head and Body

Copyright © 2024 Douglas H. Knight. All rights reserved. Except for brief quotations in critical publications or reviews, no part of this book may be reproduced in any manner without prior written permission from the publisher. Write: Permissions, Wipf and Stock Publishers, 199 W. 8th Ave., Suite 3, Eugene, OR 97401.

Cascade Books
An Imprint of Wipf and Stock Publishers
199 W. 8th Ave., Suite 3
Eugene, OR 97401

www.wipfandstock.com

PAPERBACK ISBN: 978-1-5326-9389-2
HARDCOVER ISBN: 978-1-5326-9390-8
EBOOK ISBN: 978-1-5326-9391-5

Cataloguing-in-Publication data:

Names: Knight, Douglas H., author.

Title: Worship and eucharist : the whole Christ, head and body / Douglas H. Knight.

Description: Eugene, OR : Cascade Books, 2024 | Includes bibliographical references and index.

Identifiers: ISBN 978-1-5326-9389-2 (paperback) | ISBN 978-1-5326-9390-8 (hardcover) | ISBN 978-1-5326-9391-5 (ebook)

Subjects: LCSH: Lord's Supper. | Church. | Theology, Doctrinal.

Classification: BV825.3 .K55 2024 (print) | BV825.3 .K55 (ebook)

MARCH 4, 2024 8:51 PM

"Unless otherwise indicated, all Scripture quotations are taken from the Holy Bible, New International Version®, NIV®. Copyright © 1973, 1978, 1984 by Biblica, Inc.™ Used by permission of Zondervan. All rights reserved worldwide."

Contents

Preface | vii

Introduction | ix

This Book in Summary | xiii

1   The Church Worships | 1

2   Worship in One Church | 23

3   Many Churches | 49

4   The Church and the City | 89

5   The Church for the Long Term | 134

Endnotes | 183

Index | 185

Preface

I have been very lucky with my teachers. Professors John Zizioulas, Robert Jenson, and Colin Gunton were Christians and wise men. They passed on the teaching with a directness that came from being unafraid. By exploring the way of life and thought of early Christians, they found intellectual treasure and conceptual rigor, and they avoided the morass of modern Christian thought. They shared their teaching with me over many years, and what I learned from them I pass on to you. You can be sure that the credit is theirs.

Thomas F. Torrance, Robert L. Wilken, Oliver O'Donovan, and John B. Webster have also been long-term influences and allies. Douglas Farrow and Rod Dreher have spelled out how our modern societies have been drinking from poisoned wells and, now full of toxins, are losing their mind, and becoming vicious, cultic, and totalitarian. For many decades before he became Pope Benedict XVI, Joseph Ratzinger provided the most scripturally and pastorally convincing theology of what the church has to submit to and endure in order to be witness to the world. Our identity is made known to us by our progress through the Scriptures, which, set in order for us by the church year and lectionary, reveal a Christian mind and way of life formed by this shared way of the cross.

Kent Warner has also been a good friend. He has pushed me to set out again the deep assumptions and principles of the first generations of the church that John Zizioulas has offered us. By cutting ourselves off from our roots, maybe we Western Christians are more deeply damaged than any of us realizes. Perhaps this is why it is hard for us to grasp that the future of our society depends on a church of persons who fearlessly pass on the whole gospel. We can no longer assume the good will of our contemporaries, particularly those in governments and universities. We have to fall back to more strongly defined positions, from which we can make absolutely clear that, by setting out this Christian revelation, we stand for the dignity of mankind against all his detractors and haters.

All these teachers have been good to me, so I commend them to you. I have not provided footnotes or bibliography, but if you want to know more about the origins of what you read here, you will find references and explanations in my earlier book, *The Eschatological Economy: Time and the Hospitality of God*. I am very grateful for Church House Publishing for permission to reproduce lines from *Common Worship* and *Common Praise*.

Introduction

WE ARE MADE FOR life with God. And we are made for life with one another. It is God, only, who makes life with others possible. In Christ we are brought into relationship with God and with all mankind in God's communion. This relationship comes to us as sanctification, which is made possible by our salvation. Since this makes us glad, we gather together and say so. We give thanks, and this thanksgiving is what every church service is.

The first Christians gathered on the first day of the renewal of creation, the morning of the resurrection. On each new Sunday we celebrate this new life, and we take part in all the forms of service and ministry that the resurrection of our Lord makes possible. We worship at any time, of course, each day, morning and evening, in groups or by ourselves. But when the whole congregation is present, the unity of all Christian worship and life becomes clear and public. Each service is an installment in our transformation into a holy people, and reveals that this transformation is underway.

This book takes a look at the service of worship as a public act. Here we learn how Jesus identifies with the church, his body in the contemporary world. The Lord leads his people, making us his witnesses and taking us through the challenges that will make us ready for life with God.

There are regularities to any service. As long as they have worshiped, Christians have observed that the basic course of each service reflects the descent in which God comes to us in Jesus Christ, and the ascent in which Christ takes us to the Father. By looking at its stages we discover that the gospel gives us the logic of each service. The gospel that gives us the news about Jesus Christ also gives us the news of our own true identity. It tells us about this identity in words and, drawing us together, it transforms us into this new identity. As we follow Christ we move together, both through the service and outside it. Individually and corporately, we are learning to represent Christ more truly to a world that, though it does not know it, is looking for him.

Each chapter of this book deals with the six themes of gathering, hearing, singing, praying, eucharist, and whole people. "Gathering" deals with the calling of each Christian into the event of the Christian service and membership of the community of the church. "Hearing" deals with Scripture, witness, judgment, truth, and discipline. "Singing" deals with worship, the Holy Spirit, the gifts given to the church, and with the resurrection. "Praying" deals with intercession, confession, and forgiveness of sin and then with our public role with society at large, with the secular sphere, and so with politics, economics, and culture. "Eucharist" deals with our embodiment and materiality, with our being made holy, with Christ's sacrifice, and with the bread and wine. The last theme, "Whole People," deals with the people we meet in church, with the holiness of the church, and how the whole church looks forward to its redemption.

Our worship consists of all the words spoken by the congregation and its leaders, our formal and informal prayers, and everything we sing. We will look at the psalms, hymns, and songs we sing and the prayers we pray in hope of learning from previous generations of Christians. We want to worship with increasing understanding and discover what we have been given, so that, as we pass it on, we may receive more.

All Christians are witnesses. This becomes clear when we are out together in public acts of worship, so we will look at open-air processions and festivals. We will look at the traditional forms of worship, old hymns and new worship songs, and at singleness and marriage. We will see how the service is the fundamental form of Christian mission, and how it gives rise to many other forms of Christian ministry. In a traditional church we may be surrounded by the visual aids used by previous generations of Christians who worshiped here before us. If we learn how these images and patterns communicate the gospel to us, they will no longer seem strange. We will grow by discovering that many generations have passed Christ on to us, and as we receive their insight, gifts, and service we will be able to give our witness just as they did.

Throughout the book we show how Jesus identifies with his body in the contemporary world. He is our head, and for the sake of the world around us, we are his body. By the Holy Spirit, we act as go-betweens for those who need to be reconciled to one another. We intercede for our society, speaking up to those with too much power on behalf of those with too little, and we participate in Christ's continuing passion for the world. We take up the sin and unfinished business that clogs all human relationships and bear it back to God for its redemption.

Jesus leads us through the world. As his body, we are the puzzling way in which Christ makes himself present to the world. He is available in this way so that the world is entirely free to decide whether to receive him or not. The unglamorous appearance of Christians and our ambiguity about church is essential to the freedom of the world to decide for or against Christ. As it makes its decision about him, it decides its own destiny. We can learn how to be faithful even when the culture around us does not welcome the Christian message, how to avoid becoming conformed to that society and how to bear the costs of this discipleship.

In the course of our service and worship of God we are growing up into our full stature as people in communion with God, and through him, with one another. We may learn to see each other as his, and to see the glory of Christ shining through all his people. As we become witnesses of this transformation we become a joyful people, who give thanks to the Lord every time we gather before him.

The first three chapters of this book are easy to follow, each adding a little to the previous chapter so the effect is cumulative. There is more in chapters 4 and 5 that might not be so obvious, but the first chapters provide the justification for it. Here I set out an account of the eucharist, of sacrifice, and of the presence of Christ that comes from Scripture, and from the long reflection of the whole church on that Scripture, and I show how our account must be faithful to all the acts of Father, Son, and Holy Spirit, who are preparing us for life in their communion. Much basic Christian insight on sacrifice has been jumbled, suppressed, and ignored, but here I try to set it out in plain fashion. So that you can see immediately what is going on in this book, I will put a list of points at the end of each chapter to sum up what has been said.

This Book in Summary

1. Christ is the whole Christ, head and body. The whole Christ is a central Christian doctrine. It has been neglected, and Western Christians and Western societies have suffered as a result, alternatively putting too much emphasis on the individual against the crowd or the crowd against the individual.

2. We cannot talk about Christ as though he were severed from all relationships, without his company and his glory. We can speak the truth about ourselves when we understand that our identity is created by the relationship that God has with us.

3. Christian worship is public. It takes place where anyone can see it, hear it, and join in.

4. Christian worship is the dialogue of heaven with earth. It is continuous, nothing can interrupt it, and earth depends on it for its life. In it, Christ speaks for us, and with him, we learn to speak for one another.

5. We are created to be social. The gospel teaches that mankind is made for others, and so it tells us about our life together as Christians in the holy community of the church, and in the world of communities and nations.

6. The truth about us is protected by God. Many want to regard us as the inert object of their knowledge. But God gives us life and freedom, a future and hope, so we are neither completely predictable nor knowable. Our mystery and dignity are secured by God.

7. Mankind worships, unstoppably and inevitably. Human beings cannot prevent themselves from directing their love and praise in one

direction or another. Worship is not something that Christians do, but others do not.

8. Christians send their worship and love deliberately in the one direction to the one who can return it to them and sustain them in an ongoing conversation and relationship. Others send their worship and love in many directions. Since the world is full of worship, it is not secular, but cultic.

9. The public witness of the church means that some services take place in the open air in the presence of large numbers of people. Christian worship is observed and overheard by the society around it.

10. The revelation of God is simultaneously God's revelation of humanity, and so it is the revelation of each of us to all others. God reveals that we can be truly known when we are known as creatures of God, who have been given unlimited dignity and sovereignty.

11. Christian worship warns rulers not to overstep the bounds of their authority and so prevents them from tyrannizing over their people. Christians sing warnings to rulers and encouragement to those ruled.

12. It takes all Scripture to set out the doctrine of the eucharist in its fullness and to avoid clumsy formulations made with contextless notions of presence and absence. The doctrine of the eucharist requires an account of our being made holy, our sanctification, which happens through time, and so we need an account of the consummation of humankind and creation, which is the goal of time.

13. Christian worship sustains the communities of family, city, and nation on which all others rely. It brings judgment and truth and so preserves a society from becoming fearful, totalitarian, and deranged.

I

The Church Worships

1. GATHERING—TOGETHER IN ONE PLACE

Every Sunday morning Christians gather together to worship God. We go because God calls us. He brings us face to face with one another, and sets us free to worship him. The Lord rouses us out of our everyday existence, and so we leave home, travel across the neighborhood, go up the steps, into the church, down the aisle, and take our places next to each other. When we say that we are going to church, we mean that we are coming to this gathering of people in this city who worship God.

Imagine that the church is in the center of town, on the marketplace, where everyone can see us arriving. Imagine that our service starts on the steps outside the building, or imagine that the walls of the building itself are transparent, so that services are visible to everyone in the streets outside. Everyone in town can come and listen and join in. Every church service is a public event.

Worship Begins

By gathering together here, we have answered God's call, and come into his presence. Where two or three are gathered in his name, Christ has promised that he will be present and hear them (Matt 18:20).

The service might start with the words "The Lord be with you," to which we reply "And also with you." We can say these words, or sing them. The Lord speaks, and we may hear him and reply. He speaks and we respond, and he hears and responds to us. The whole service is a conversation between him and us, God and mankind.

The Christian people worship God only, no one else. In their worship they proclaim that the God of Jesus Christ is the only one worth our praise. This makes us distinct from every other community.

The community sings: "Glory be to God on high, and in earth peace, good will towards men." All humans receive glory from God. It is this glory that makes all human life possible, for it allows us to recognize the worth of one another. God has given us his recognition, and we pass it on to one another, and then back to him.

We cannot help giving our worship and adoration to someone. If we do not give ourselves to Christ, we give ourselves to something or someone else. We want recognition, and we throw ourselves on anyone and anything in order to get it. Only if we direct all our worship to God, are we no longer desperate to receive recognition from any source or at any cost. As we worship him, we receive all the recognition we want, and become secure enough to pass it on and to recognize and affirm other people. God's affirmation is the currency of all human relationships.

God loves us. He has called us into existence and he loves what he has made. He knows who we are, and glories in us, and the glory we receive from him is truly ours. Of all the many things you are and might be, God is able to recognize what truly belongs to you and what does not. We have no need to hold on to glory for ourselves, or to pass it on in any direction to which it does not belong. When we worship, we are not so much giving glory to God as giving it *back* to God, from whom it comes in the first place.

God gives you your glory. He secures your identity, finally and forever. The truth of your identity is found within a relationship of love, in which there is freedom. When we return this glory to God, we acknowledge that he knows us and loves us truly. As we acknowledge God, we also affirm that we receive our true praise from him, and we are able to acknowledge all other beings for who they are. We can know them and love them, rightly and truly. This saves us from giving our adoration, and ourselves, away to the wrong recipients.

When you receive your identity from God, you find your place in a communion in which you are cherished. Outside it, there are endless threats to your identity, which you have to defend yourself against. But within that communion, you are known and loved, your identity is established, and you are saved. Then we are able to be glad and thank God. When Christians gather, and become visible as the church, they give thanks, and their thanksgiving is what Christian worship is. We say that we are both obliged and delighted to recognize God's grace to us; we are glad and we express this. So, we say, for instance: "It is indeed right, it is our duty and our joy, at all times and in all places to give you thanks and praise, holy Father, heavenly King, almighty and eternal God, through Jesus Christ your Son our Lord."

Brought Together

The people who gather together here are essential to what is going on, for the church is made up of those who turn up. Simply by gathering his church, God makes the church distinct from the surrounding world. He makes it *holy*. God gives Christians his holiness in order that they can live in his company and be his witnesses to the world.

By faith, the church says that these people are holy. We may see how ordinary we are, and the rest of the world may only notice how inadequate we are. But we cannot look past these Christians to find the holiness of God elsewhere, for God has given them the promise of the resurrection and determined to make them his holy people, the church.

We may want to play down this difference between ourselves and others, but there is no reason to do so. This distinction between the church and the world is fundamental. By calling these people together, God maintains the distinction between the church and everything else, and he does so for the world's sake. The church has its own enigmatic identity, which allows the world to recognize it as the community that always raises the question of the truth of the world.

God gathers us into the communion made by his love. This company of people is the circle within which we may discover love. Since we receive the love of God, which is without end, we can afford to love each another. We do not need to drive hard bargains and calculate payoffs. Within this communion, we have an endless supply of love and, with it, forgiveness by which we can allow each other a new start. This communion makes itself known through the fellowship of the church. The love of God comes to us in the form of a specific fellowship of people being made holy by God, in this fellowship in which our true worth and identity are being revealed. This love expresses itself in this public act of worship, and this is what is being declared to the watching world each time Christians gather together in church.

2. HEARING—THE WORD OF THE LORD

Scripture Is Read

Christians gather together in order to hear the word of God. God has promised to speak to us through Holy Scripture. Every time we meet, the Bible is opened, and read, and the gospel is heard.

A passage from the Bible is read out loud, slowly and clearly, so we can all hear it. Week by week Scripture presents us with the whole dealings of God with us in Jesus Christ. We hear three readings, from the Old Testament, and from an epistle and from one of the four Gospels. In the Old Testament we hear the testimony of the patriarchs, prophets, and people of Israel, and we respond to the testimony of this first group of witnesses by singing a psalm of praise to God. Then comes the epistle, the testimony of the first Christian communities that came into being as the witness of Israel spread across the world. We reply to this second reading from the epistle with a hymn.

Then comes the gospel. Jesus Christ himself is the gospel, the fulfilment of the promise made to Israel and then to the world. As we read from these three parts of the Bible, we hear from three sets of witnesses, and in their words, God speaks to us. The word of God comes to us whether or not the Bible has been well read; it comes to us through the clear and confident, or the stumbling and self-conscious, delivery of the reader. Scripture read in church is the act of God, speaking live to the world, and making himself heard here and now.

God addresses us. We can hear God because Christ has heard the Father and responded on our behalf. Because Christ heard and has answered, Abraham was able to hear and to answer, and Abraham's "yes" to God brought into being a whole people who could hear that call and answer the same way. Abraham, Isaac and Jacob, and Moses and David were all able to answer because Christ heard the voice of the Father and made their response for them. Peter and John and the other disciples were able to hear because Christ heard and answered for them, and enabled them to hear and answer too. God has called and mankind has answered. God's call to mankind has created this community on earth that has heard God and waits for him to speak again.

God speaks and mankind hears. God knows us and can tell us who we are and what we may become and asks us if we are ready for this identity offered to us by witnesses. All Scripture, and only Scripture, gives us this vast account of our identity as the people of God. The particular passage that is read out to the assembled people is the word of the Lord for today. As Scripture is read, we hear the words of Christ. We hear "Come to me all you who are weary and burdened and I will give you rest" (Matt 11:26), and "I am the way, and the truth, and the life. No one comes to the Father except through me" (John 14:6), and "Do not let your hearts be troubled and do not be afraid" (John 14:27) and "Take heart! I have overcome the world" (John 16:33).

From Scripture we learn that it is good news that Christ is Lord. We are not the master here, and we may not turn other people into our servants. He releases us from our panicked grip on one another, and from the burdens we load onto one another. Christ commands me to let you go. He tells us that we have acted like little tyrants, but that we may do so no longer. We must concede that it is so, and that our negligence and abuse of others, and our delusion about this, may not continue. The uncaring masters are dismissed and the poor are released. This is a relief, for the poor but also for those who have oppressed them. But it is also a traumatic event. The word of God comes as judgment on us and so it comes as a shock.

The Sermon Opens Scripture to Us

We have gathered to hear the word of God. First this word is given in the reading of Scripture and then it is opened up for us by the sermon, which repeats in other words what we have just heard, showing us how these readings from Scripture are connected. We learn that Christ is the fulfillment of the promise made to God's people in those Old and New Testament readings. The sermon reminds us of last week's readings, so that we follow the people of Israel in the Old Testament, and we follow Christ and his apostles in the New Testament, and through the weeks, we see the continuity of the word of God. Scripture gives us the narrative of the events that make up the life of God's people, integrated in the gospel of Jesus Christ. The sermon tells us that this history of God's people is also about our own future life with the people of the Lord, for we may become part of this testimony of God to us.

The sermon may also draw our attention to elements of the service, such as a verse of a hymn, or our responses and prayers, that reveal our identity within the people of Christ. It can point out events in the life of our community, in the church year, in the parish and the borough, and national and international events and, by integrating all these into the narrative of God's people, the sermon shows us how we may also become witnesses of God.

The Name of God

We have heard Scripture and the sermon that opens it to us. In affirmation of what we have heard, we say the Creed. We stand and say, "We believe in one God the Father Almighty, Maker of heaven and earth."

The Almighty Father, who made heaven and earth, has called us, and given us a name. He calls us "my people," and each of us "my beloved," and as a result we receive our particular Christian name from the church in baptism. In replying to God, Jesus calls him "Father," which gives us the name "Father, Son and Holy Spirit." We may look for another less unilateral and controversial name, on which we can all agree. But "Father, Son and Holy Spirit" is the identity that the Lord has given us. This name has been secured in the Creeds and has to be taught and learned, just like all the rest of this faith. Not everyone likes this, or agrees with it. It is not too obvious to need saying and that is why we have to say it, in this creed and preaching. We who confess it in public worship do so with our hearts in our mouths, which is just as it should be. We are the community that, by God's grace, is able to say "This is the Word of the Lord" and "Thanks be to God."

3. SINGING—MADE FREE

When Christians come together, they sing and give thanks to God. We sing because we have been made free and, like calves let out of their stalls after a long winter's confinement (Mal 4:2), we are enjoying our new freedom. The whole Christian body feels this release and expresses its joy in song. From the Prayer Book we sing: "O Lord, open Thou our lips," and we respond with "And our mouths shall shew forth thy praise." We sing sentences and acclamations. We say "The Lord be with you," and we reply "And also with you." We say "Christ is risen" and we reply "He is risen indeed. Alleluia." We say, "Let us bless the Lord," and reply "Thanks be to God."

These Christian acclamations have come down to us from the earliest days of our faith. If you ask us to say in simple terms what we stand for, we can do so. We can confess the whole mystery of faith in a single line: "Christ has died, Christ is risen, Christ will come again."

We sing because Christ has freed us to do so. With our singing, we join our voices to worship that is already ongoing. This worship is his before it becomes ours. Every Christian worship service is a participation in the Son's worship of God the Father, so with these songs and hymns we are able to join in with the Son, and hear the Father's reply.

The worship service is also Christ's *service to us*. Christ speaks and intercedes for those who cannot do so for themselves, singing songs of lament and of thankfulness alternately, on behalf of all mankind. Christ stands at our head, while we stand behind him and sing along with him, so we can cry with those who cry, and sing with those who rejoice when their crying has been heard.

The Glory of Jesus Christ

Jesus is *Christ*, that is, *Anointed*. He has been anointed lord and king. The Holy Spirit does this anointing. He makes Christ king *for us*, so that he is *our* lord and *our* Savior. The Holy Spirit makes Jesus known to us, but he also keeps him beyond the reach of our knowledge. In the incarnation, the Holy Spirit put Jesus into our hands, first as this infant and then as the Lord who acts as our servant. But then he raised him, for the resurrection took Christ out of our power again, and set him at the right hand of God the Father.

Now we have been put into Christ's power. We are in his reach, but he is not within ours. We may know him on his terms, but not on ours. When the Spirit gives him to us, we may know Christ and confess that he is Lord; but when the Spirit does not do so, Christ remains beyond our power of perception. He never becomes the involuntary object of our knowledge and power. The Holy Spirit always glorifies Christ, so that, in this holy company, we may know him as Lord, and as *our* lord.

The Holy Spirit brings us into the presence of Jesus Christ, here with all these others, and so makes us part of his company. He brings all opposites and rivals together, reconciling us to one another, creating peace between us, and enabling us to recognize one another as members of one body.

The Holy Spirit reveals Christ to us, bit by bit. He conceals the whole glory of Christ from us so that we may receive only as much of it as we are ready for. He gives Christ to us in the form of intangible packets of holiness, the various characteristics that we call the gifts of the Spirit—"love, joy, peace, patience, kindness, goodness, faithfulness, gentleness and self-control," in the list that the apostle Paul gives (Gal 5:22). The gifts of the Spirit build the body of Christ. That is, whatever gifts you receive from the Spirit are given to you so that you can exercise them in service of the rest of us, so we all benefit from them. We learn how to be patient and long-suffering with one another, and we grasp that these people, whom we do not find attractive by nature, are the intimations of himself that Christ has sent us. The gifts of the Spirit describe Christ, but they also describe us as we will be, joined with him. As the Spirit brings us together, he turns us from in-turned beings to people who can love and live in truth.

For the sake of the world, we are drawn into this public event of the gathering and reconciliation of all parts of the world. The Holy Spirit animates this congregation, made up of these different age groups and backgrounds, to sing and pray. Our worship is an echo of the worship of heaven: it started before we arrived, continues after we have left, and goes on uninterruptedly out of our earshot. Christ presents the world's worship to God and we are caught up into this act. With him we can say: "Lift up your hearts," and we can reply, "We lift them up unto the Lord."

4. PRAYING—SPEAKING WITH GOD

Christians gather to pray and intercede. Since God has spoken to us, we can speak, and he waits for us to do so. We learn the story and songs of the people of God in order to know what to say. Then we may say what we like, and ask for what we want. All our prayer is formed by the prayers of previous generations, starting with the first whose witness we receive in Scripture. They have passed on to us the songs and prayers to use for every eventuality, the psalms in particular giving us the words to pray.

Christian worship makes us an articulate people, who pray and speak up for one another.

The Lord Hears

Jesus speaks up for us and says what we do not know how to say for ourselves. He carries our prayers to God, and so he is our spokesman and representative.

The way the Lord Jesus addresses God is the only way in which we may speak to him, so we are now the people who may address God as *Father*. God has spoken to us, and now, because he has spoken, we can speak. Having spoken, God listens and waits for our answer, for he is *our* Father. "His disciples said to him, 'Lord, teach us to pray.' He said to them, 'When you pray, say: "Father, hallowed be your name. Your kingdom come"'" (Luke 11:1–2). This prayer has been the basic form of all our prayers ever since. We have been given the name to call and have the promise that God will listen. In Christ, God is in conversation with mankind, and as a result, mankind is in conversation with God.

Because Jesus prays, we may do so too. He prays so that we can hear and follow. "Jesus looked upward and said, Father, I thank you for having heard me. I knew that you always hear me, but I have said this for the sake of the people standing here, so that they may believe that you sent me" (John 11:41–42). He teaches us how to speak to God with all directness. "So, I say to you, Ask, and it will be given you; search, and you will find; knock, and the door will be opened for you. For everyone who asks receives, and everyone who searches finds, and for everyone who knocks, the door will be opened" (Matt 7:7–8; John 11:9–10). "Give, and it will be given to you. A good measure, pressed down, shaken together, running over, will be put into your lap" (Luke 6:38).

The whole Christian service of worship is this prayer and conversation with God. Nonetheless, one part of our service is called "the intercessions," in which we pray "for the Church and the world, and thank God for his goodness." We pray together and for ourselves: we may acknowledge our own neediness, and we may ask for justice and blessings for others. We pray for those who are nearest to us, perhaps starting with family, friends, and the people we work with. We can pray for the patience or courage to sustain us through the challenges we face. We can pray for success, at school; at exams; at work; for promotion; for love, health, and wealth; for all our worthy and unworthy desires together. We ask the Lord what we should do within each of these relationships and pray for those gifts of the Spirit, that will enable us to make the right decisions in each of these places.

As we speak, we can raise whatever issue is on our mind. We can ask the Lord whether he will be always be faithful to us. We can charge him with being unfair. We can speak up for those who are unable to speak for themselves, or who only know how to blame or be resentful. We may indeed blame God for everything that is wrong. We can protest, but we do so in hope.

The Lord expects us to tell him what is wrong. To point out to God that many people await justice and that there is great evil is a faithful, not faithless, thing to do. In our prayers we ask God why things are the way they are, and lament that things are not yet right. The church laments, and it can only do so properly in faith, hope, and love. In faith, we can ask God how his project of life with mankind can possibly work. We can ask, because we are certain that he is worth asking and that there is an answer worth having.

The Lord speaks gently and patiently to the world, and to us, and he waits for us to answer. He listens and intends that we not only listen to him but also to each human creature. God intends us to become listeners, who can respond to the prayers and requests that we make of one another and learn how to give a hearing to everyone who calls us. Anyone, no matter how humble or far away, may expect to call anyone, no matter how important, and get a hearing from them.

How to Pray

We *learn* to pray, to give thanks, and to look forward to the kingdom in which we will share. We may ask for his provision. We may ask for the forgiveness of sins and release from all trouble. The pattern we know best are the Lord's prayer's seven petitions: hallowed be your name, your kingdom come, your will be done, give us our daily bread, forgive us our sins, lead us not into temptation and deliver us from evil.

We pray with others, and we learn from them how to pray. In the service there is an alternation between prayer leader and people that allows us all to join in and to speak in unity as one people. We learn to pray with our whole body, so for example when to kneel and to stand, and we come to know all the prayers of the service by heart. Prayer has its own logic and so it has regularity. We begin formal prayers with a one-line summary of what God has done and what he has promised that tells us who we are talking to and what we may hope for from him. We constantly have to be reminded to raise our sights and to ask for more. We call these "collects," the long-used prayers you find in the Prayer Book, which gather up and summarize the prayers of the whole congregation.

5. EUCHARIST—ONE BREAD

Eucharist means "thanksgiving." We receive our life from God, and we acknowledge this with thanks. Giving thanks is the way we deal with everything that comes our way. Thanksgiving is what is most fundamentally going on in any Christian worship service, as it is through all Christian life. In each service Christ ministers to us, and we express our joy at finding that it is he who is doing this. He gathers us together, brings us into his company, and is now at work making us members of this *communion* that is *holy*.

We have heard Scripture, sung songs of praise, and prayed. Now bread and wine are carried up to the altar. When he has received them, the minister prays the eucharistic prayer of offering: "Blessed are you, Lord, God of all creation, through your goodness we have this bread to offer which earth has given and human hands have made. It will become for us the Bread of Life."

The minister prays that, whatever we bring, the Lord will take it from us; that is, whoever we are, and whatever condition we are in, the Lord will receive us. Christ lifts mankind to God, and God receives mankind from Christ. God has taken hold of mankind, holds him now in a relationship that is eternal. In this eucharist, Christ lifts us back to God and holds us in their communion, and the Father receives and affirms all that the Son lifts up to him.

The eucharist is also an offering made, and a gift given, to us. At the Passover supper celebrated with the disciples in that upper room, Jesus took bread, gave thanks, broke it, and gave it to them. So here and now, he brings us in, sits us down, breaks this bread and gives it to us. He feeds us and waits on us. The food he offers us comes from this creation that he has prepared for us and placed us in. Piece by piece he gives this creation to us, breaking it and opening each piece for us. He serves us himself, and he sits at this table and eats with us, so we become his equals. Though broken, we are made whole simply by being this close to him. He gives us these installments of this creation, and simply by choosing them for us, he makes both them and us holy. So, we say, "happy are those who are called to his supper."

The words of the eucharist remember the past event of the passion of Christ. We remember that our Lord, "in the same night that he was betrayed, took bread and gave you thanks; he broke it and gave it to his disciples." In this remembrance (anamnesis) we look back to those events, for they brought into being the future which we now look forward to.

The Last Supper

We look back through his incarnation, passion, and death by remembering—re-living—the Last Supper in the upper room. Supper with the disciples was followed by the garden of Gethsemane, Jesus's arrest and trial, his being scourged, stripped, dragged out of the city, out of all human society, and put to death on the cross. We call all this the "passion." It tells us how deep the incarnation is: God's relationship with us goes all the way down to the very bottom of human existence. It shows that God really has met mankind and stayed with him and that, since not even death can undo it, this is irrevocable. The passion is the unchangeable fact of God's dedicating himself to us. The incarnation is the being of God with mankind. Because we and all disobedient powers oppose it, the passion is the form that the incarnation takes.

Jesus is handed over. To show that, in this way, God is handing himself over to man, Jesus hands this bread to his disciples. As this bread is in their hands, so the Son of God is in the hands of man. Christ is about to be broken and divided up, so he breaks and divides this bread. "He took bread and gave you thanks." He performs this handing over and being broken up in miniature, demonstrating what was to happen, and showing that it happens with his consent. It looks as though it is by his own power that we are taking Christ into his hands to do something appalling to him. It may seem as though Jesus is simply the victim. But, by playing this all out beforehand, Jesus shows that, though our violence is let loose, we are not master of this event at all. It is Christ who gives the instruction to "go and do what you are going to do," to Judas (John 13:27). He took this role in it for himself, so in these events in which he seems most passive, he is entirely active and willing: he is *actively* passive. It is not Judas, not the crowd, not the Sanhedrin or high priest or Pilate who are in charge—but the Lord.

Our time here and now in this eucharistic service, is superimposed on that moment then. All the events that followed the Last Supper—the Mount of Olives, the garden, arrest, passion, and crucifixion—are played out in this supper. Through this meal the entire incarnation and passion of Christ are on display. The eucharist superimposes the events of the Lord's passion on our time, so that these two times are playing in parallel. Our time, and the time of that Last Supper, are brought into sync in the eucharist. As a result, we are able to follow Christ and to watch this offering and giving of God to us from a distance. Our response is, "Praise to you Lord Jesus Christ. Dying, you destroyed our death. Rising, you restored our life. Lord Jesus come in glory."

The Body Calls together the Scattered Fragments

Christ breaks open this bread for us. He divides it up and hands it over to his friends. He is doing this opening and handing over. God places himself in our hands, so God is really given and mankind really receives him. Nothing else can break him open, indeed, nothing in all creation can even leave a mark on this indivisible loaf. He gives himself. But this division and opening is not the only thing going on here.

Whether we are aware of it or not, each of us brings something to the eucharist. Imagine that, as we reach the altar, each of us empties our pockets of whatever fragments have accumulated there during the week, each crumb representing some event in which we have been involved. We are these fragments. Now imagine that we put them together on this altar, and at once these fragments combine together to form a single loaf. Imagine that this "one bread" is a large round unleavened flat-bread. Then this eucharistic bread, the "Host," is lifted up so we can all see what has happened. God has called us from all corners of the world, and gathered together to make this one loaf, held up by the minister so we can all see. Those fragments have been replaced by this wholeness. This loaf is us, in Christ. We are the first batch of the new creation. As we say in the eucharist: "Though we are many, we are one body, because we all share in one bread."

The Body Opens to Let Us in

Two things are going on at once. The first is that this loaf is that community, and that community is the indivisible Christ: we are part of him and he is one of us. The loaf is the church, that is to say, all other Christians. We must grasp them and cling on to them. Joined to each other, we are integrated into this body that is Christ's.

The second thing is that this bread opens to let us in. The indivisible divides: the loaf opens himself. He shares himself with us, and as we eat what he gives us, his strength floods into us and makes us pure, indivisible and unbreakable. The Holy Spirit, the indivisible and indestructible, divides and distributes himself to us, making us a single indissoluble people, each of us increasingly holy and unique. What he has given us is his own indivisibility. These two things have to be said about the bread of the eucharist. As we say in the service, "We break this bread to share in the body of Christ."

The Opening and the Passageway

Now there is a third thing that must be mentioned. This loaf is our way into the future world. This loaf is the doorway into the kingdom but, like the "eye of the needle," it is so narrow that no created thing can get through it. Since we cannot pass directly through them, all created things are barriers which we can only pass by going around them. But for the Spirit who created them, no created thing is a barrier; he may freely pass through any creature, for they are all as penetrable to him as the air is to us. Any and every material thing may open to let him through when the Lord approaches it. But for our sake it is only these specific things, bread and wine, that have been nominated to be this doorway because, in the Last Supper, the Lord used them, and commanded us to follow him in using them, in this way.

The Holy Spirit passes through these eucharistic elements to us. These specific elements of creation through which the Spirit comes, bring Christ to us, and identify him for us. We meet Christ here, where this word, this Scripture, and these eucharistic elements of bread and wine are. We say: "Gather into one in your kingdom all who share this one bread and one cup."

6. WHOLE PEOPLE—ONGOING SERVICE

Let us take a look at the service as a whole. The Christian people is gathered together to hear, sing, pray, and be made the body of Christ. As the people arrived, they were greeted by the gospel, the word of God. The Lord led them up the aisle of the church to the altar where they were received from him in the eucharist by God the Father. Then the Lord leads them down the aisle of the church again and out into the world, in order to travel through the world as his envoys.

To see this action at its very simplest, imagine that a large round loaf is raised above our heads, that we all move towards it and become part of it. This is the first movement that we see in the service. At the climax of the eucharist, the minister holds up the loaf as Christ lifts up his people and, in his hands, we are that loaf. We stream towards it until we become integrated into it, and there our future with him becomes briefly visible. Then, in a second movement, this people stream out from that loaf into the world, each of us is then a portion of that loaf traveling through the world. This ascent and descent is the basic pattern that the people of God play out before the watching world.

Sending out

At the end of the eucharist the minister turns to the congregation and says: "Go in peace to love and serve the Lord." This is the commissioning and sending of the people to the world, sometimes referred to as the "dismissal." We are made the envoys and apostles of Jesus Christ, given our mission and sent off to carry it out. We travel through daily life, speaking to all in the person of Christ, exercise his mercy, judging for ourselves where gentle words, and where hard words, are needed.

The worship service does not come to an end, but is simply taken out into the world. Each Christian is the Christian worship service, live. Each is the whole worshiping assembly in miniature carrying that worship with them. Through the week the members of the body take the service and communion of God out through the world. We say: "Send us out in the power of your Spirit to live and work to your praise and glory."

We have looked at the church service through this pattern of gathering, hearing, singing, praying, and eucharist. There is a logic to those stages that reflects the way in which Christ comes to us and takes us to the Father. But the eucharist is not always the explicit culmination of a worship service. The service may build up to the ministry of healing, in which there is an extended confession, people are prayed for, and there is a process of identifying our wounds so that the healing process can begin. Or the service will end on the sermon, which either teaches the church or, if people have been invited to hear the gospel for the first time, which may call people to repent and be converted to Christ. These ministries of praying, healing, teaching, and preaching are aspects of the one indivisible ministry of Christ to us. In all these different forms of service, Christ serves us and ministers to us.

At the end of the service members of the congregation often gather at the back of church to talk about the various forms of ministry that this service now takes them to. It may take us visiting, bringing communion to people in their homes, taking people to visit other members of their family. It may take us to school, to the night shelter, to hospital and prison visiting, fair trade campaigning, and to the youth group and summer camp. And we talk about the jobs we do in the week in the hope that we may be witnesses to our colleagues at work and that the work we do, however commercial it is, provides a service that adds something to the common good. All of these are outworkings of the service.

Uninterrupted Service

Each Christian is the church and speaks for the whole church. We speak by blessing, thanking, and talking up whatever we possibly can. In the offices in which we work we ask our colleagues to act with as much generosity and imagination as they can, to judge well, for the widest good and for the long term. We intercede and petition for those who have received no hearing. We lament when sections of this society remain unheard, and we point out that, when some are unheard, our society as a whole is impoverished.

We have been brought together to participate for a moment in the celebration that takes place uninterruptedly before the throne of God. When we come together, we are brought into the unbroken time of God. This week's service is not ultimately separated from next week's service by six weekdays, for secular time does not divide what the Spirit holds together. Christ does not go off-duty, but is forever our servant, always here for us, so the six days of the week are an outworking of the seventh day of the unbroken service of Christ for the world.

We are being called into a great company. The whole world is invited to watch and take delight in Christ's service and to come into this great assembly and participate in his work. Before us the Lord reconciles the apparently irreconcilable and brings all things into communion so that they become ready and willing to receive each other. Our particular congregation is part of the communion of God that is visible in this place and that is therefore witness to God for the world.

What Can We Learn in This Book?

In this work I want to give you what the whole church has always taught, which has served Christians for many centuries. You will have to try out these insights for yourself and see if they fit with what you know. Since you are a Christian, you have a feel for what is good and true, and for what is in line with what you have been taught. You know that the gospel is "the message of the cross" (1 Cor 1:18), and that this means that we will keep running up against the world, often have to disagree with it, and part ways with it. You know that this is costly and requires courage. You know that an easy form of discipleship is always on offer, but that a gospel without the cross has no power. It is down to you to tell the difference between the easy way and the real way, and this means that you have to test what you hear or read to see if fits with Scripture and with your own Christian experience.

In this book I talk about the gospel and the people who spread it at the same time. The gospel makes its own communicators: it makes us speak, and it speaks through us. The gospel travels from past to present to future by transmitting itself person to person. In this book I assume that the gospel is not only communicated by one Christian talking but also by many Christians, talking and singing together. We not only speak one at a time, but also voice our experiences together, in unison and in harmony. The gospel is communicated as much when we are singing and praying as when we are preaching or teaching. It is not only the proclamation of one preacher that carries the gospel but the speech and act of the whole company. When many Christians speak and sing simultaneously, their unity may persuade anyone who is listening that what he hears is compelling and true. What they hear is not simply a list of truths but the whole action of many willing people acting coherently together. It is not simply about speech but also about the slow and deliberate large-scale movements of people responding to the worship that is always going on in heaven, and responding to others as they listen to that worship too.

The Christian worship service is therefore a complex interplay of people communicating and acting, so that at any time, some are making their contribution, others listening and considering, and then adding to it, in a stately sequence of alternating responses that reveals the depth of their listening and replies to one another. They honor, and defer to, one another in this way. Together they communicate that they are listening to Christ's high priestly worship of God the Father and to the worship of the whole company of God gathered around him. Their listening to, and relaying, this heavenly liturgy is the way the gospel communicates with the world.

In our worship, Christian people are responding to the action of Christ. Though for us Christ is offstage, how they respond to him can be seen by those watching and listening, who may deduce for themselves that Christ is leading and his people are following. Our Lord is initiating this action; we reply and imitate him and act in concert with him. We can, because he enables us to do so; what we do and say are not simply our acts but his, his power enabling ours.

The gospel is not simply a matter of ideas and information but also a matter of power. It is not power only, but a new relationship that restores what is broken, brings truth, and gives life. It is not only true, but it is the truth itself; the truth himself brings us into truth. This relationship is the exercise of power, but exercised so patiently, over such lengths of time, that we do not notice it as power at all. The gospel brings life, and it is the life it brings; life brings itself to us, and gospel is what we call it when this happens. But this is not simply life, but it is a particular person, who places himself before us.

We do not just communicate verbally, or through reading and writing. We communicate with images and words together; an image helps us to grasp these words, and these words help us grasp this image.

When the community meets it is an image of a much larger community. This image comes into view when you see this gathering from above. When you are looking down, perhaps from an upper window or from a hillside, and you see this assembly as a single body, it forms an image of the unity of Christ with us. As the people of this community move about in response to one another and to the Scripture they hear, they form a series of images of Christ coming into creation, bringing salvation to us, and making us his people, and so creating that unity. Many images appear and follow one another, noticed only by those who are listening to the Scripture, and they all amount to this one image of the unity of God with mankind in Christ. Even before they start speaking, these people are, as they stand, a picture of the reality that God is bringing into being—they can be this picture because in small part, they already are what they are becoming. They are the beginning of the reality that will grow before our eyes and become increasingly obvious. They are able to portray it because they are a first installment of it, and each part is identifiable as a miniature version of the whole. This is the result of the very gently exercised power of God to make it so.

This is not a book simply about ideas but about persons moved by the words and power of Christ. It is about the movements of great numbers of persons together, in ways that are visible and comprehensible even at a distance. The watching world can grasp something of who we are and what we are doing, even when it is out of earshot and its attention is engaged by other things. The people of our neighborhood are taking something in, long before they are willing to admit it and before they are ready to stop what they are doing, come over and listen.

If it is to be useful to you, this book has to offer you something that, though they may not realize it, many modern Christians are missing. The first thing to realize is that it wasn't missing for the first generations of Christian. They had it, we need it, and we can learn it from them.

Our individual uniqueness is established by God and revealed by the gospel. But when our pursuit of individuality decays into individualism, it means that we are cutting ourselves off from lasting love and real life. Many communities claim they will assist our individuality, but only baptism into Christ, and so the gospel with the cross in it, can stop us pursuing those things that cut ourselves off from life. In those first generations, people feared being cut off, and they understood salvation as being grafted into a community that existed long before they joined it. And they knew that it was this community that gave them their value, and that the apostles and saints were their friends. Our sin, and other people's sin, cuts us off. The result of sin is isolation and atomization, and when sin has its way, we die. Death is being cut off finally. When Christ grafts us in to his body, those who had been nobodies became somebody. They knew they were members of this community that reaches from the throne of God down to earth and that overcomes all the damage humanity has done to itself. Salvation is belonging, life lived together within the holy company of Christ's body.

Perhaps we need to reexamine our belief that only individual communicators use only words to speak to an audience that is already prepared to sit and listen. It is this individualist assumption that the gospel is a matter of words only, spoken by one person at a time only, which has stalled our progress in the Christian life. When many people speak and sing together, they are also proclaiming, communicating, and moving, approaching and responding to Christ.

The next thing that is an obstacle to the growth of discipleship is ignorance and suspicion of most of the generations of Christians before us. We have received the gospel because they passed it to us, each generation teaching it to the next. They did so by teaching the songs, copying the Scriptures, explaining what they say, printing the Bible, and publishing the books in order to pass this teaching on. This chain of transmission was never broken. Every generation was faithful enough to make the effort and investment in passing the gospel in all the depth of its teaching on until it reached us.

I think this should interest you, because like me, you come from a culture that believes that the only way we communicate is when someone is prepared to listen to a speaker giving a talk. Our assumption is that communication is either top-down, one-to-many, speaker to audience, or it is one-to-one, a private conversation. The modern church has stalled because of this assumption that has separated us from the church of other centuries. They knew that communication is not solely verbal and written and that we are not solely individuals sitting on our own before texts. We are members of one body, because our Lord brings us together as such and puts his worship in our mouths. This is the insight we are going to explore in these chapters, the truth of which you are going to judge with the wisdom you gather from all the Christian witnesses placed around you.

Chapter 1 in Summary

1. **"Church" means the people who gathered around Jesus Christ.** It is the assembly of those worshiping God truly.

2. **The gathered Christian community is the people of God and the body of Christ.** Christian witness is embodied and made present by a particular body of Christians. God brings them together so that the world may see this gathering and wish to be part of it.

3. **When we discover that, in Christ, God has committed himself to our service, we are thankful, and this thankfulness expresses itself in our worship.**

4. **Christian worship comes down from God to mankind and then returns back from us to God.** When we sing and pray, we are taking part in this second movement, from mankind to God, from earth to heaven.

5. **Each worshiping congregation relays the worship that takes place in heaven.** When we join the worship of that company, we relay its gladness to the world around us.

6. **Worship of the true God breaks us out of imprisonment to our own idolatry.** If we do not worship the true God, we create substitutes for him, worship them, and become trapped by them.

7. **The Lord speaks to his people through the word given in Scripture.** He relays to us the voices of the witnesses of his holy people. The many books of the Bible contain the statements of many witnesses, gathered by God to speak to us, each in his or her own voice. That these many voices give us this single testimony is demonstration of its truth as the single indivisible testament of God

8. **His commitment to us does not threaten God in any way.** He is not prevented from coming close to us by concerns for his own power or holiness. His power does not prevent him from being gentle, but enables him to be gentle. He does not overpower us.

9. **Each Christian can pray and speak to the God of heaven of earth.** They can speak and pray for all those who do not speak or pray for themselves and so can act as the intercessor and mediator between mankind and God.

10. **Those who were scattered are gathered together to become one body.** Though mankind has become broken, humanity may be reintegrated in the company of Christ's people.

11. **With the Spirit, Christ makes us members of that body that he is presently alone.** Having made us whole, Christ present us as such to the Father.

12. **The Holy Spirit delivers and installs in us the gifts and abilities of Jesus Christ.** Each gift, and each Christian, serves the whole body.

13. **The Holy Spirit gives us the holiness of Christ and purifies us from what is unholy.** Our progress through the world, and endurance of its opposition, is the way he purifies us.

14. **The Spirit supplies the truth of the world to us in installments.** We receive in doses the redeemed world within which we can develop the character and practice the action of Christ.

15. **The Holy Spirit makes this public assembly vocal and articulate so that it may speak and pray truly.**

2

Worship in One Church

WE MAY LEARN ABOUT Christian worship and witness by following the church service. In this chapter we observe one church, listen to its prayers, and so notice the pattern and logic of its worship.

1. GATHERING—IN THIS PLACE

The People Underway

On Sunday morning the people of my church gather together. The service starts with the entrance hymn (Introit). As we sing our first verse a procession appears from a side door at the front of the church. It is led by a dozen people wearing white surplices over robes. The first person in this procession carries a large cross, the second and third carry large candles, a fourth carries the Bible, then comes the priest and deacons. Notionally this procession leads the whole congregation, so we follow them, singing a hymn, such as:

> All people that on earth do dwell
> sing to the Lord with cheerful voice
> him serve with fear, his praise forth tell,
> come ye before him and rejoice. (William Kethe)

The procession comes down the side aisle, turns at the back of the church to go up the central aisle and up to the front, where each of them takes their place. The rector sits on a seat behind the altar, the others on one side or another. We dress these people in white to remind ourselves that all Christian people are promised radiant new garments of holiness.

Christians gather in order to make this journey together. We form a cavalcade. Although at different times in the service we are sitting or kneeling, we are nevertheless on this journey right through the service. This community of a hundred people is led by this little procession of people who are themselves led by the cross and word of God. We are singing versions of the psalms that the people of Israel sang as they journeyed up to Jerusalem, the city of God. Our first hymn echoes these songs of the journey and of the ascent to the house of God, so they are all about coming into the presence of God.

On the Street

We are a people on the way. We make our way across the borough in order to be here together. At least a couple of times a year our service begins outside the church. We are led by the same little group that heads the procession, dressed in these white garments, and we follow the cross and torches that they carry.

In this way, on Palm Sunday, we follow our Lord up to Jerusalem and into the city for the final week of his passion. On that morning we meet in a square in the middle of the borough, with Christians from other churches, and pray and sing with them. Then we process back to our church, singing:

> All glory, laud and honor
> To thee Redeemer King
> To whom the lips of children
> Made sweet hosannas ring.
> (St Theodulph, "All Glory, Laud and Honor")

People come out of shops and cafés to listen and watch. Our worship is not confined to our church building, but is audible, visible, and public.

The Glory of the True God

The next thing we sing in the church service is the Gloria: "Glory to God in the highest, and peace to his people on earth." This has inspired the most complex musical settings, but in our church we all sing it together, to a simple tune, with some gusto.

> Lord God, heavenly King,
> Almighty God and Father,
> We worship you, we give you thanks,
> We praise you for your glory.

We worship God because he has made himself *our* Lord. The result of giving this glory to God, and not to anyone else, is peace to God's people on earth, and for this we give thanks. We confess that the God of Jesus Christ is the only God, and that he, and no one else, is "most high in the glory of God the Father." We bear his name to the world, and we bear the world to God. So, we sing that the God of Jesus Christ is the only God, "For you alone are the Holy One, you alone are the Lord, you alone are the Most High, Jesus Christ, with the Holy Spirit in the glory of God the Father."

When we give glory exclusively to God, we can recognize all creatures for what they are, the intriguing and marvelous creatures of God. Worship of God is the backstop that prevents us from taking too low or too high a view of those around us, so that we do not demonize or idolize them, but give them the proper regard that they are owed.

The confession that only God is God takes place in the face of all the many claimants to divine status. There are rival gods and alternative authorities, but we declare that none of them are what they claim to be. Other people give themselves up to all sorts of powers and forces, but Christians are content to remain with the God who gives them life. We take our lives from God and are renewed by him.

Why worship God?

In its worship the Christian community says that the Father of Jesus Christ is the only God. We say this because other "gods" are vying for us. Maybe no one calls them "gods," but when claims to power are left unopposed for so long that they are beyond challenge, they have become effective gods of our society. We have to refute their claims and tell their makers that they are not gods, and not beyond challenge. There is competition for control over us, spiritual warfare, going on (over our heads perhaps), through all our politics and culture, and through all our daily lives and encounters. It is for us to challenge those who want us to believe they are unchallengeable, and this is just what Christians are doing when they sing glory to God alone.

In our public worship we return all glory we receive back to God. When this glory is not returned to him, it becomes identified with various ambiguous imperatives and authorities that withhold it. Such unchallengeable "forces" and "gods" emerge so gradually that it is difficult to see how they have done so. There are many "more-than-human" powers and subhuman powers, and their effect is always to us make less-than-human. We inherit these from previous generations, and we inflict fear of them on one another. They are the bad debts that the generations that come after us will have to face. The ancient world called them "gods," and the Christians of the early generations called them idols, evil spirits, or demons, and this is how we should regard them. Worship of the true God rids us of these, and so in the traditional terms, it is a purification, an expiation, and an exorcism.

God makes a community that acknowledges him as God, and that refuses to recognize anyone or anything else as divine. This community identifies him as the provider of all things and gives him thanks for them. It does not see them as threats that we need to fear. We worship God so that we do not become enslaved to anything that is not God. We remain safe when we receive all things as his creatures and his good gifts. "All things come from you," we say, "And of your own do we give you."

It is only confession of God that prevents us from making our own claim to divinity over other people. The church is public witness to the world that this is so. This community is put here by God to stand in the way of all others claims and form of partisanship, and to stand against all the half-truths that are promoted into all totalitarian claims. This service is the church's public confession that there is only one God. He is the one true reality, and the sole anchor for all other identities. He is his own master, and so impartial and utterly on our side. We cannot manipulate him, and he cannot be drawn into our conspiracies. God is not dependent on our worship. He does not need anything from us, and so cannot be warped or corrupted by flattery. He does not allow us to attach our various projects and partisanships to him, for we may not "take his name in vain," misusing or abusing it (Exod 20:7) He stands up to us and prevents us from destroying whatever is good and true and putting our own transitory inventions in their place. He alone is God, and he is God *for us*, and we are happy when we know this.

2. HEARING—WITNESSES OF GOD

By listening to the word of the Lord in Scripture the people of the church become his witnesses.

The Presence of the Word of God

The word of God comes to the world, and the church hears this word and receives it for the world.

In the Sunday morning service, the Bible is carried into the center of the church. It is held up high so everyone can see and hear it. As the gospel is read out, we greet it as Christ himself, here with us. We stand and the deacon says, "This is the Word of the Lord," to which we reply, "Thanks be to God." The gospel is read and the Lord is heard. The Lord speaks to us, live, in the words of Scripture read out in the church service. These words of this particular reading are his word to us now, in our unique present circumstances.

The Bible was part of the procession that entered the church as the service began. In that procession, the Bible follows the cross, and is accompanied by the two candles or "torches," the lights of the Old and the New Testaments. These two testaments are "two witnesses who agree" (Deut 19:15). We visualize them as the two cherubim who wait on the Lord and his people, day and night singing "Holy, Holy, Holy." Behind the deacon who carries the book of Scripture comes the minister who will open Scripture and interpret it for us.

Before the gospel is read, the Bible is brought down from the altar. The deacon turns about so that the open Bible faces the minister. The minister swings the censor over it so that puffs of incense rise above the pages of the Bible. This incense makes visible to us the holiness of the word of God contained in this testimony. What will the Lord God say? What glory will be revealed? A gospel sentence is spoken: "Speak, Lord. You have the words of eternal life." The priest says: "Hear the Gospel of our Lord Jesus Christ according to Mark," and we reply "Glory to you, O Lord."

When the Scripture is read, we hear the words of the Lord and are in his presence. Since we read from at least two parts of the Bible, so we hear from at least two witnesses. We are reminded of them by the two light-bearers, one for the Old Testament and one for the New. We hear the Old Testament, and we reply with a psalm. Then we hear from an epistle, and we reply with a hymn. Then the gospel is carried down from the altar while we sing "Alleluia," and we hear the gospel. From the Lord we receive instruction, encouragement, and warning. At the conclusion of the reading, the minister says, "This is the Gospel of the Lord," and we reply "Praise to you, O Christ."

The Bible leads the procession back up to the altar, while the minister makes his way to the pulpit. Perhaps nothing as deliberate and formal as this is done in your church. The preacher simply goes to the lectern or to the microphone. But whether we are aware of them or not, the same elements are there. In the deep memory of the church all the movements of the gathered people, led by the word and the cross, trace out the path of Christ into the world and the path that we take as we follow him, his descent to us and his ascent to God with us.

The minister climbs up into the pulpit and says something like "May the words of my mouth and the thoughts of our heart be now and always acceptable in thy sight." He acknowledges the awesome responsibility of this moment, for he has to pass on to us what the Lord says to us.

The reading of Scripture and its interpretation in the sermon are fundamentally the same event. The word of the Lord is opened for us. The scroll is rolled out and what is written there is explained to us. Isaiah put it this way: "One of the seraphs flew to me, holding a live coal that had been taken from the altar with a pair of tongs, the seraph touched my mouth" (Isa 6:6–7). Ezekiel heard an instruction and followed it: "Mortal man, eat this scroll, and go, speak to the house of Israel. He gave me the scroll and . . . in my mouth, it was as sweet as honey" (Ezek 3:1–3).

The sermon tells us what we have heard in these three readings. It connects these lessons together, and relates them to previous and future lessons. It draws our attention to the whole action of God for us as it is laid out in the reading from Scripture and in all the psalms, hymns, songs, and prayers that make up this service. It explains how these relate to each other and so how the whole service of Christ and people form a unity. The sermon is not an interlude in the worship, but gathers together the Scripture and the worship of the church to show that they are saying the same thing. By spelling out the relationships between the readings, it indicates where the church presently is and what it must now seek in its prayers.

As soon as we have heard this Scripture, we respond to it by singing and praying. Our worship, hymns, and prayers have accumulated as the response of the church to Scripture. In my church we follow these in the form set out in "Common Worship," the collection of worship services set out by the Church of England, along with a hymn book and book of worship songs, and you do something similar in your church.

The Word of God Sustains the Church

The Bible is made up of many books, containing many statements from a "great cloud" of witnesses (Heb 12:1). The Lord has gathered this company so that they can speak to us, each in his or her own voice. It is for our sake that they went through their trials and their experience was written and passed down to us. That these many voices give us this single testimony is demonstration of its truth as the indivisible testament of God. Since Scripture gives us the testimony of these witnesses of the action of God, it is our foundational document, our constitution.

The word of God we hear week by week gives us the gospel through the year. Our church reads the Revised Common Lectionary, which is followed by the Roman Catholic Church, the Church of England, and many other churches. This lectionary establishes the passages from Scripture that we are going to read over the course of the year, and indeed of each three-year cycle, and so it ensures that we read the whole Bible. It sets out the minimum that we are going to read, though it does not prevent us from reading more. It is our curriculum or syllabus. This week's readings follow those of last week, so that week by week we are following a trail through Scripture that takes us through each book of the Bible. In this way we are not only able to celebrate Christmas and Easter at the same time as every other Christian church, but Advent, Epiphany, and Pentecost too. The significance of each of these festivals becomes clear through their relationship with each other.

Everything here is said to the Christian people: all this Scripture is for the church and, through the church, is it for the world. The church service is a public place in which all questions are heard and anyone may bring an accusation against anyone else. No one is too powerful to be challenged, no one too lowly or inexperienced to speak. All that is secret is revealed here. Any church that fails to hear and pass on the word of God will betray the community to which it is sent. The church is given to the world so that the world can watch the church hearing, or failing to hear, this word.

3. SINGING—WITH ONE ACCORD

Gathered together in worship, we are in the Spirit, and so in the presence of the Lord. The Spirit brings us out of isolation and into communion with God and with all creation.

The whole company of heaven speaks and sings. Their service started long before we arrived, for this crowd in heaven has worshiped God from its creation. Their celebration spills over to us and makes up the service of worship in which we participate. Their singing precedes ours, and their acclamations are what we hear in the worship every Sunday. "O come, let us sing to the Lord; let us heartily rejoice in the rock of our salvation. Let us come into his presence with thanksgiving and be glad in him with psalms" (Ps 95:1–2). This company looks forward to our coming.

The whole company of heaven sings, and we sing back, so every service is made up of this call and response. The Lord speaks to us in Scripture, and his company respond in the sung replies to that Scripture, and our voices participate in their replies. As we sing together, we become of one mind, with each other and with the Lord.

We pray, "Lord have mercy, Christ have mercy." This is the pulse of every church service. In Greek we sing *Kyrie eleison*, in Latin we sing *Domine miserere*, and in English, *Lord have mercy*. In all Christian worship we declare that we have received mercy and then we ask for more. In all our worship we ask God to give us what is good, and to show us how to receive everything with thanks so that we are able to receive everything that comes from him as good.

We sing out of a sense of relief. By worshiping God, only, we are freed of all other forms of worship. We acknowledge that, though there are many forces and pressures on us, none of them deserves our worship. Our release from them has been announced, and our worship is our response to this news. So, we sing, "My soul magnifies the Lord, and my spirit rejoices in God my Savior. He has brought down the powerful from their thrones, and lifted up the lowly; he has filled the hungry with good things, and sent the rich away empty."

This is the song of Mary as she declared herself willing to receive the Savior for us (Luke 1:46–55). The Lord lifts up the neglected and demotes the arrogant. We sing this canticle, the Magnificat, at Morning Prayer and perhaps sing the hymn version of it, "Tell out my soul the greatness of the Lord," at the eucharist.

Worshiping with Heart and Mind

Our thanksgiving has a basic pattern that each service at in my church follows. This is set out in "Common Worship," the form followed by the Church of England. We call it "Common Worship" because it enables us to worship in common, that is together. We do not sing or pray singly, but in unison and harmony, and the result is that we, and anyone who hears us, can understand what we are singing and giving thanks for.

Our worship must be intelligible, Saint Paul tells us in 1 Cor 14. We sing and speak so that people can understand what we are saying, though we worship God, and we also lead and teach those worshiping with us how to worship and what to say. That is to say, the worship itself gives us its reasons and so explains itself as it goes along. Our worship consists of short phrases, like "Lord, have mercy," and the repeated phrases that make up worship songs. And it consists of long sentences with complicated syntax that make up hymns. We need both the full account and the acclamations that sum it up. The sermon points out how our songs reply to the Scripture we have heard, so we notice what we are singing, and sing with our minds as well as our voices. Though we are many different minds, personalities, and voices, we are of one mind. As the whole people increasingly speaks and sing, with one voice, each of us truly gains his or her own voice for the first time.

Every service book or breviary is a long chain of passages from Scripture, adopted by the church from its earliest days for its worship. With all its prayers, sentences, and responses, it puts the words of God in the mouth of the whole congregation, where they can "dwell richly" (Col 3:16). Psalms give us our response to each passage of Scripture, and hymns give us our response to the psalm. We need all these three elements of Scripture, psalm, and hymn. We need the sermon to point out to us the connection between Scripture, psalm, canticle, hymn, and worship song, and we need someone who understands the Scripture and the psalm to choose the right hymn, that continues the theme that appears in Scripture and psalm. Just as there are several readings from these various communities of witness of the Old Testament and New Testament, we respond to them with different sorts of song, the psalms from Israel, the hymns from the church, and the briefer contemporary worship songs of our own generation. So together we all "sing psalms, hymns and spiritual songs" (Eph 5:19).

The Spirit Gives the Body Its Voice

The Holy Spirit brings us into his fellowship, which is the communion of saints, here for us. This communion is love, embodied as these persons. It opens us up to love and mutual service. The Holy Spirit brings us into the body of Christ, which is the love of God given to the world. The Holy Spirit is how the Lord is serving and securing his people, glorifying Jesus by uniting his people to him. The Spirit has been sent to us to act as our helper, who is literally "on call" (*paraclete*). We have only to ask, and he will come and teach us to speak with the Lord. He will not give us what we cannot cope with, so no absolute power is put into our irresponsible hands, but he will enable us to ask for what we need.

The Spirit comes with gifts that build up the body of Christ. The gifts given to you are to be exercised by you in service of the rest of us. You exercise them on our behalf. They are our gifts because they are yours. The canticle from Isaiah lists some of these: "The Spirit of the Lord shall rest upon him, the spirit of wisdom and understanding. The spirit of counsel and might, the spirit of knowledge and the fear of the Lord" (Isa 11:2–3).

The words of the Son are set in us by the Spirit. Their speech and life animate us, and give us our speech and life, so each of us truly gains our own voice for the first time. We are able to recognize one another as different from ourselves and let one another be so. The unity, given to us by this heavenly company, maximizes our diversity. The Holy Spirit brings us here before all these other people and holds this community together, making it one body. The Holy Spirit frees our tongues so that we can sing. He holds us together as a single worshiping body and so enables us to speak and sing together.

Freedom and Discipleship

Where the Spirit of the Lord is, there is freedom (2 Cor 3:17). To confess that Jesus Christ is Lord is to renounce all other masters and forms of compulsion. Having identified the Lord, the right lord, we can be fearless in the face of every other claimant to power.

The freedom of the Spirit has to be learned. He does not abandon us to our own devices; freedom comes together with this fellowship, which means with these Christians to help us and with all the practices and conceptual tools of discipleship. The guidelines, practices, and exercises of which this discipleship consists are the gifts of the Spirit. We learn to serve, to exercise restraint and to judge ourselves, and to serve and wait for one another. We exercise judgment on one another's behalf and we ask them to advise and correct us and so to exercise their judgment on our behalf.

The Spirit gives us all these other sanctified, experienced Christians, all of whom are committed to assist our sanctification. Christians are taught this more rigorous lifestyle that teaches us to turn away from some of the apparently urgent things presented to us. We cease to raise some people to more prominence than is good for us or for them. We are no longer as easily pushed about as everyone else and we gain a mind of our own, and the confidence to speak up. One of us says, "Lift up your hearts," and the rest of us reply "We lift them to the Lord." He continues: "Let us give thanks to the Lord our God," and we respond, "It is right to give him thanks and praise."

4. PRAYING—ASKING FOR FORGIVENESS

We have come to the Lord, to hear him and speak with him. We have withdrawn from the world a little and come together in order to do this. Prayer does not require that we withdraw from other Christians, but that we pray together with them. We may say our prayers without worrying what our feelings are. Sometimes habit and routine help us through; at other times our prayers are more heartfelt, said with more involvement, concentration, or even desperation. When we find nothing to say, we pray that God hears the prayers of those around us; we learn to pray our own prayers unconcernedly with them together.

Intercessions

We pray, for ourselves and for the world. Scripture, sermon, and the creed are followed by the intercessions. These may be led by members of the congregation. If this is a different person each week, their character shows through in their prayers. The whole church depends on the example of these few who know how to pray, probably because they have been taught prayers in earliest childhood and know them off by heart. The prayers might begin: "Let us pray for the Church and for the world, and let us thank God for his goodness." After each prayer, there is pause, which each of us fills with our own prayers. At the end of each set of prayers, we respond: "Lord hear us. Lord mercifully hear us."

We pray for our own community. We pray for our children, and then for all the children they mix with in school. There are plenty of children and teenagers without fathers to model themselves on; we know how angry some of the young in our borough feel, so we pray for them, their parents, whether or not they are known or absent, and we pray for the reconciliation of generations. We pray for those facing age, ill-health, and the vanishing prospect of recovery, and so we pray for the provision of care for the elderly and for the staff in hospitals. This leads us to pray for those working in health care, education, and the social services, and so we pray for our borough and city.

We pray for the world, usually starting with whatever part of the world is in conflict and so in the news. We are also linked by friendships and relationships to the church in different parts of the world, and so we pray for those Christians who we know are under pressure. And we know that they pray for us, so that we may be faithful witnesses here too. Finally, we pray, "Merciful Father, Accept these prayers for the sake of thy Son, our Savior Jesus Christ. Amen."

Prayer continues in other forms, after the service and before it. By the font at the back of our church is a prayer corner with a notice board and a stand for candles. After receiving communion some of us come to this corner in order to continue praying. We light a candle and pray for our families. Praying and lighting the candle is the same act in two forms: that candle is our prayers; lighting it and leaving it to burn belongs to the prayer just as much as stillness and bowed heads do. On the notice board people pin the names of family members who are ill or in trouble; we keep a book with these names, and these people are then prayed for by name in the intercessions.

Repentance and Forgiveness

After the intercessions comes a general confession of sins, "in penitence and faith," and the proclamation of our forgiveness.

We are one body, so none of us carries the whole weight by ourselves. If you leave me alone with my sin, I am done for. For as long as I carry it and keep it a secret within me, it wears away and hollows me out until nothing is left of me. To confess our sins is the first breakthrough. So, we confess: "Almighty God, our heavenly Father, we have sinned against you and against our neighbor in thought and word and deed . . . through negligence, through weakness, through our own deliberate fault."

To confess our sins is to give up pretending. It is good to be able to call things by their names, and not to deny that they are what they are. At the very least, sins are misfortunes. They turn more serious when we become trapped by these misfortunes and can only repeat them. Even before we get to the issue of who is to blame for them, it is good to be able to say out loud that we regret what has happened and are sorry for our part in it. We are able to admit this, because the congregation, in the person of the minister, invites us to do so. "We are truly sorry and repent of all our sins."

With this repentance comes relief. We can let go of our mistakes and allow our sins to be taken away from us so that we are freed for new relationships with others. Put your burdens down, for they do not belong to you anymore. This task is long, and requires repeated and lifelong effort. Each time we pray together: "For the sake of your Son Jesus Christ, who died for us, forgive us all that is past and grant that we may serve you in newness of life."

We ask the Lord to forgive "all that is past." We are asking him to put it in the past, where this sin is out of our reach and the reach of everyone else affected by it. Until the Lord puts it there, it is not in the past but still here, hanging around in our present, souring our relationships and hindering all our attempts to try again. Without forgiveness, each of us carries so much junk that we have slowed to a crawl, always processing but never finished with any task. Each of us is held down by the weight of unfinished business, created by those encounters in which someone got the better of us. We nurse our wounds, and consider how we may get even. But when God commands, we have to own up to this resentment and let it go. In the name of the Lord, the minister prays, "Almighty God who forgives all who truly repent, have mercy upon you, pardon and deliver you from all your sins, confirm and strengthen you in all goodness, and keep you in life eternal, through Jesus Christ our Lord."

This is the absolution. We are absolved: the ties that bound me are untied and I am released. Many people have been sinned against by me, but God has authority to act for them all, and to release them from me and me from them. The Lord has the authority and power to act on behalf of all creation and of each creature in it. It is his exercise of this authority that keeps creation open, so that it is not crushed by the weight of its own past.

We have been at war with the world, and we have been in denial about this war. Though we may not have offended these people in church, our reconciliation with those we have injured starts here. They receive this repentance and announce this reconciliation and peace. They forgive you, and they do so for those whom you sinned against who are not here to forgive you. The sign of the peace, in which we exchange a handshake or embrace, is our reconciliation with those we have offended. We turn and we shake the hand of those standing next to us and say, "The peace of the Lord be always with you," and they reply, "Peace be with you."

Judgment and Confession

The Lord God knows us. He has spoken to us and has given us his name, so that we may speak to him. As we call him and come into his presence, we become aware of our deficiency and need, and ask the Lord to have mercy on us. We confess the sin that our neediness has forced us to. We admit that we have taken praise that we should have passed on to God and so have attempted to live apart from him. We have to make this statement publicly, to him and to all. As we come into the assembly of the Lord, we ask God for his mercy and pray for release. "Almighty God, to whom all hearts are open, all desires known, and from whom no secrets are hidden: cleanse the thoughts of our hearts by the inspiration of your Holy Spirit." We ask whether we may enter his presence and hear his voice. We confess our sins to God and to one another publicly, ask God for his forgiveness, and we ask one another for forgiveness too. Then we can hope that we may "worthily magnify your holy name."

We are released from our burdens, so we can stop and put down our load. We can set down that vast bundle of obligations that we are unable to fulfill, so we may feel a huge sense of relief. But strangely, the load often has to be taken away from us because we have become so used to it that the thought that we have to let go of it is threatening. The masters are judged and taken off the backs of the poor and so the poor are released. We are those masters. To us this judgment may not come as good news.

With this declaration of forgiveness, we may approach the Lord in the eucharist. We repeat our confession and plea for forgiveness. At the eucharist the whole congregation accompanies me up to the altar. They know that I have to be rid of that unfinished business that I no longer know how to cope with and that poisons me and everything around me. When I hesitate at the back of the church, the servers beckon me down; they know that I cannot carry any more than I am already carrying. They encourage me down that aisle and up to the altar, to dump that sin. I arrive loaded down with all my hurt and fury. At the altar, at the feet of the Lord, I heave that weight off my shoulder and it disappears, as though down a chute, and is gone. I can stand up straight again and turn away from that sin. The church prays the prayer that announces that all that was outstanding against me has been canceled. By this absolution they publicly authorize and empower me to go free.

The very act of our praying is the outworking of God's act in releasing us. Our tongues are set free. We learn how to be thankful and how to be remorseful: we do not pursue these particular emotions, but they come as we learn our place in the worshiping people, and begin to comprehend the dimensions of what we are given in Christ.

5. EUCHARIST—OFFERING AND PASSOVER

Every service in which Christians gather and worship God is part of the one eucharist of God. The first half of any eucharistic service is known as the service of the word and the second as the Eucharist, respectively the ministry of word and of sacrament. The Lord himself administers these two ministries: the word brings us the knowledge of God while the sacrament brings us into communion with him so we receive a share of his holiness. But every Christian service is eucharistic from beginning to end, even when no bread is broken, when it may be termed a "worship service," "family service," "healing service," or named after some other ministry.

The Passover

The eucharist is the meeting and this provision that brings us into fellowship with the Lord. This fellowship meal is the Passover that liberates us from our bondage to death. In this event the Lord handed himself over to us, and we took hold of him and handed him over to die. There are two distinct acts of "handing over" here. Christ is handing the kingdom to us. And in the passion mankind hands Christ over to death. Christ gives us all things. And we refuse them, and hand him away as though he were of no value to us. Yet we are not able to get rid of him, for this passion is not his alone, but also ours.

The eucharist is the Last Supper and the Passover. We are not only gathered at the table in the upper room in Jerusalem with Jesus and the disciples, but we are also in Egypt with Moses and the Children of Israel at the climax of the great struggle with Pharaoh and all the divinities of Egypt. The eucharist therefore places us in the events of the book of Exodus: chapter 12 sets us in the meal that the people of Israel were instructed to eat before the Passover itself began. Just as the people of Israel were confronted by Pharaoh, so now Christ is about to confront all the forces of death that are arrayed against him and all mankind. He is going to take on the principalities and powers, and lead his people out of captivity and away from the power of death: "through him you have freed us from the slavery of sin."

With Christ and with the people of Israel, we break out and escape. We make our passage out of Egypt, the House of Death, and break through into the promised land. The eucharist is our Passover and our food for the journey. We are in captivity: before our breakout we eat together for one last time in order to gather the strength for the escape, and as an anticipation of the feast we will enjoy once we reach our freedom in the new country. But first Christ has to overcome great resistance of Pharaoh and lead his people out of their captivity to all powers, tyrannies, and forces of evil. The cross is the breakout. Christ breaks open the small and vicious place to which we have been confined, so an opening appears in the side of the world we know, and we are led out into a vastly bigger world that we had no previous knowledge of. Christ tears open the world that has been captive to death; when the bread is torn the wall that held us in is torn down. Christ is the passage through the two halves of this bread and so he is our way out: we escape through him as though down a new-discovered passageway.

Secondly, Christ carries us out. He can do so to us because he himself is entirely unhampered. He has no sin and no needs of his own. He is the lamb who "takes away the sins of the world." It should be a beast of burden such as an ox or a donkey that carries us, or carries our pile of ordure away from us. A lamb is no beast of burden, but it has the characteristic of being conspicuously innocent. He has no violence whatsoever within him, no guilt, no taint of other people's blood, and so he is utterly innocent, like a lamb. We pray, "Lamb of God, you take away the sins of the world. Have mercy on us." Since the lamb has no burdens of his own to carry, so there are no constraints on his power to act for us, so he can do for us whatever we cannot do for ourselves. His power is unlimited and so he is able to carry us.

Christ Offers, and Provides, All Things

The eucharist is the *offering* of Christ. In my church the servers bring the cup and paten up to the minister at the altar. The minister takes them, lifts them up and gives thanks for them. We lift creation and our fellow human beings up to God. We are able to do this, and our minister is able to do this, simply because this is what Christ does for us, and enables us to do for one another.

While we sing a hymn, known as the Offertory, the servers bring the collection up in a basket and take it up to the altar. In our church there is no passing a collection bowl around. You can drop whatever you want into a box that stands in the aisle, but you are quite free to overlook it. You do not pay for us: we pay for you. The minister receives the collection dish. He prays that the Lord will take whatever we bring and take us in whatever condition he finds us. Then the minister receives the bread, wine, and water that have been taken up to the altar. The offering is comprised of the bread and wine and the money given in the collection. This is the offering which "earth has given and human hands have made."

In this Offering, or Anaphora, two things are happening. One is that Christ carries us to God and presents us to God as his very own body. And God accepts us and receives us from him. In God's view, we are his. The second is that Christ is being presented to us. We can decide whether we will accept him and receive him, which means that we also receive each other as his people and his creation, and accept them as members of his body. If we receive this eucharist from him, we receive the forgiveness and salvation that he holds out to us. In these two ways God gives himself, and in Christ he takes us and holds on to us forever.

From beginning to end the whole service is this eucharist that draws us from all corners of the world into the presence of God. We have seen that the service starts with the procession in which we are drawn, out of our homes and work, through the streets of this city and into church, and finally up the aisle to the altar. At the altar, the priest holds up this single loaf that we are becoming part of. Christ has drawn us together and now holds us together, forever: at this moment in the eucharist the priest is Christ, and we are the bread that he raises before the watching world. We are the harvest that Christ has gathered and worked, and which he now presents to the Father and which the Father receives from him.

Christ has set himself to serve us and free us from all the other masters to whom we give ourselves away. He supplies what we need in order to make us complete. We are the offering that he is going to present to God. Christ is the giver, we are being given, and God is whom we are given to. Christ provides for us, and the whole world is that provision. He brings us in and feeds and waits on us. What we need, he has provided. All our daily bread and material support comes from the creation that he has set out for us. He offers it to us, we have begun to receive it, and are able to give thanks. He has done all things necessary so this atonement is full and sufficient.

Those Who Were Scattered Are Gathered into One Loaf

Christ gives us the church. He gives each of us this indestructible fellowship and communion, and he makes each of us a part of it. The priest who holds up the disc of the eucharistic bread shows what is happening here. Where we see the priest and this loaf, there is Christ, making himself locatable for us. Christ is here, in this way, for us. We process up towards this loaf that he holds out to us, we enter it and become integrated into it. We are the many fragments which, brought together, are made into this loaf. All opposites are united, the disunions of the world are overcome, and all that has been divided now becomes indivisible. So, following a theme of the very earliest eucharistic teaching of the church, the "Didache," we sing: "As grain once scattered on the hillsides, was in this broken bread made one, so from all lands thy Church be gathered into the kingdom of thy Son."

The bread is the life of the people of God that are given to us through the Scriptures. Since wheat is harvested and milled, bread represents something that is broken. "Bread" includes the sowing, cultivating, harvesting, threshing, milling, baking and serving that nourishes our bodies and "makes glad the heart of man" (Ps 104:15), a combination of natural process and human input, that "earth has given and human hands have made." This bread is distributed, as Christ has handed himself over to us. But this bread also represents what is unbreakable, an indissoluble unity that will remain for us forever. It is the body of Christ with all his people, glorified together in this holy communion.

The Christian community is a single indivisible loaf. "There is one loaf," the apostle Paul says. "We who are many, are a single body, because we share this one loaf" (1 Cor 10:17). We are being made that pure and indivisible entity which nothing can pull apart and which we will therefore never be separated from. The bread that the priest lifts up is an image of this unity. Just as we grasp that bread, we are grasped and held by the whole body of Christ. We eat and internalize this bread and just so the body receives us. The Gospel of John makes this just as palpable as it can be: "*chew* on my body," Jesus says (John 6:53). We should bite down, chomp on him, and not let go. Christ has grasped you and he will never let you go; now we can do what he does, so we may grasp him and hang on. The powers of this world want to tear us off, chew us up and swallow us down. But since we are integrated into our Lord, they cannot get their teeth into us or consume or assimilate us. We are part of that loaf in which our indivisibility is established forever. Nothing will ever break down that unity or separate us from it. We will come back to this theme in the last chapter.

The loaf is the church, which is to say, it is all other Christians. We must grasp and hold on to them. Joined to them, and clinging to each other, we are being made this one body. This bread identifies the place at which the body of Christ is starting to come into existence. Perhaps we should not say that the *breaking* of bread, but the *coming-into-existence* of the indivisible loaf of Christ and his people, that is the center of the Eucharist. "Through him you have made us a people for your own possession."

Many Gifts

Christ dispenses himself to us gently. He is always able to give us more, but he does so patiently, waiting until we are ready to receive more from him. He gives himself to us piecemeal, through time, and we call these pieces, sacraments. Sacraments are installments of holiness. One installment after another enters us, each preparing us for greater relationship with Christ and his people by making us holy. If we are willing, each is integrated within us and we are further integrated in this holy body of Christ. Altogether, the sacraments make us holy. In this bread and cup is all the holiness of Christ, portioned out so that, given time, each of us becomes able to recognize Christ and to recognize one another as holy and belonging to him.

Christ not only supplies us with what we need but frees us from all that we do not need. He takes our misdirected worship, our half-truths and our unfinished business, and he sends it back to God for its redemption. He is able to pick up our sins and take them away from us. He is the beast of burden who is able to carry away whatever we cannot bear so that it disappears over the horizon with him, from where it cannot bother us again. Christ keeps us in good order. He gives us these gifts and takes our sin away: this is the "wonderful exchange" he performs for us.

The whole service of Christian worship is eucharistic, since where Christ is, his people and all elements of creation assemble to give him their thanks. Where he is, all opposites are reconciled, the fragments of this world are united, the divided become indivisible, and there is the indissoluble communion formed by his love. We hold up for the world the one bread that is us with him. This indissoluble unity, this holy communion that is eternal, gives itself to us in these installments of holiness. Each of them is a little packet of resurrection, and each enables us to "look for the resurrection of the dead and the life of the world to come." Our life consists in discovering what we have been given and giving thanks for it.

6. WHOLE PEOPLE—SENT OUT INTO THE WORLD

When we are gathered together in worship Christ reveals himself to us and he reveals us to one another. He reveals that we are his and that he is ours. When we call him "Lord" and "Christ" we mean that he is *our* king, lord for our sake, so that we stop being at war with one another and may become members of a single realm.

In the church we meet one Christian after another. As we receive them, and discover that it is Christ who is giving them to us, we learn who he is. Christ comes to us first in the form of these Christians whom we meet here in the church service. Christ gives himself to us, but these Christians are the form in which, for now, he does so. By the long slow process of sanctification, week by week, we change from in-turned beings who are afraid of other people and defend ourselves against them, to persons who are able to receive every other human being as the kindness of God to us, and so to take them for our own.

The Commission and the Uninterrupted Procession

We who have been gathered together are now led out. Our Lord sends us out into the world, to "live and work to his praise and glory." At the end of the service the minister says, "Go in peace to love and serve the Lord."

The one loaf divides and disperses into the world. We see this Spirit-filled people flow out from this loaf into the world. They appear from that loaf, descend from the altar, come down the central aisle, out of the church and into the city. We see them led by Christ, identified by the cross, the candles, the deacon carrying the Scripture, followed by the minister and the congregation. From this loaf the procession of God's people streams away in all directions into every corner of the world, bearing their witness, for they are the form in which the communion of God comes to the world.

For the next six days the church is less visible. Though we are that single body, we are in many different homes and places of work. Like seeds we are scattered and dropped into the ground. But though we are in different places, we are not separated, because space and time are not finally able to divide what the Holy Spirit holds together.

The Christian people are sent out by Christ, they journey through the world, and they return back to him again. The Lord sends them out and he calls them back again, to be refreshed, so that they are always on the way out and on the way back. "Exitus-reditus" is the traditional term for this pattern of going out and coming home, which we see in the descent and ascent of Christ who "humbled himself . . . therefore God exalted him" (Phil 2:8–9). The service and witness they offer to the world will only remain good as long as they regularly come back into the assembly of Christ's people to be renewed. As they go, each Christian is the whole worshiping assembly and uninterrupted service of God in miniature, for the assembly can divide into as many little assemblies as there are Christians, each of whom takes the whole service of Christ with them wherever they go. The single Christian cannot be detached from this company of saints, because the Holy Spirit binds each one of us to all the rest. Each is the whole procession in that place, making Christ's people visible there for all who watch, both for those who turn away and for those who are drawn in.

The Generations of Christ's People

Jesus presents us with the people we find here in church. They are his first gift to us and we have to receive them from him. We even have to receive them as Christ himself. This is not to say that we should try to see through them or past them. Their very individuality with all its awkwardness is the gift of Christ to us. The way to Christ is through the Christian life lived with them. We can see the people in the rows around us, but behind them, presently beyond our vision, are many other rows of Christians who belong to the whole company of heaven.

In many churches you see an array of people portrayed on the walls and in the windows. There are the images above the altar, and in the carvings above the choir stalls, in the glass of the windows, in paint, fresco and mosaic all around the church. In the windows of my church, you can see Christ in glory, and below, Jesus carrying the lamb that is his emblem, framed by Mary on one side and John on the other. In other windows there are other figures from the Old Testament and all the apostles from the New Testament, and from the subsequent history of the church. They are all looking towards Christ and pointing us towards him. These pictures give us a preview of the many encounters with the people of God who are ahead of us.

Many church buildings are covered with images of the patriarchs and prophets of the Old Testament. But when the prophets are not portrayed in full, they are represented by the single figure of John the Baptist, and the people of Israel are represented by the single figure of Mary. These figures gathered around Christ reflect his glory and radiate his holiness. All these witnesses are now urging us on.

Christ Raises Us

Christ is with God, so mankind is with God. This is the new truth of our humanity. All mankind is made for the society of God, that is, to be as free for God as God is free for him. God has determined that mankind will be free. We may not extinguish our freedom: all his attempts to give it away will be unsuccessful. We may wish for something less than life with God, but there is no other life for us to have.

Christ has been raised. He is the head of this body: what is true of the head will be true of the body too. The whole people will be raised. The church is the anticipation and the pledge of the resurrection. The unity of Son and Spirit, demonstrated by the resurrection, holds all these otherwise incompatible persons together in the love and communion that is the church. They mediate this resurrection to us, slowly, so that it may be internalized within us.

The Spirit keeps us joined to Christ, and he keeps Christ distinct from us. He holds Jesus out of our grasp, beyond the power of our perception. Christ is here by the Holy Spirit. We are present to Christ, but the Holy Spirit hides Christ from us and reveals him to us only in the least obvious way, bit by bit, in the form of the many persons of whom this community, the body of Christ, is made up. As we are made holy, we may realize that it is indeed Christ who is being revealed to us.

At the resurrection you and I will finally be fully turned outwards towards one another. We will no longer be cut off from each other, but I will be raised to you, and you will be raised to me. The resurrection presently makes itself known to us, again by faith, in the resurrection of Christ and in the existence of the church. The church is the thin end of the wedge that is the kingdom of God, inserted into the side of the world to open an imperceptibly small crack. What is visible of this wedge is the church, but the church is the gap through which the whole communion of God comes serially and gently to us, in time.

God has raised Jesus Christ, one of us, to the full stature of humankind. In Christ the whole work of creation has been successful, and that success is opened to all of us. Through the Holy Spirit Christ has attached us to himself, so that the resurrection of the first of us is the beginning of the resurrection of all humanity. Easter is a preview of the consequences of this for us: Christ's resurrection is a rehearsal for ours. For this reason, we say, "It is indeed right, it is our duty and our joy, at all times and in all places to give you thanks and praise, holy Father, heavenly King, Almighty and eternal God, through Jesus Christ your Son our Lord."

Chapter 2 in Summary

1. **The church is the assembly of witnesses by which the world may see its salvation and in freedom receive its life from God.**

2. **Christian worship takes place in public where anyone can see and hear it, and join in.** The gathered Christian community is the body of Christ making itself available in that locality.

3. **The church worships God in order that we remain his people and do not become prey to other gods and forces that are unable to help us.** Christian worship saves us from all other forms of worship in which we are tempted to fear and obey whatever malignant creatures, institutions, and ideologies wield excessive and destructive power.

4. **The word of God calls into being those who bear the gospel.** Christian worship broadcasts the whole gospel. In each service Scripture is read out loud to any member of that society that cares to hear it. From the Bible we hear the many voices and statements of those whom God has made his witnesses. The church follows the narrative of the incarnation and passion of the Lord through the worship service. Then it takes that same witness through the world.

5. **The whole company of heaven sings, and we sing back, so every service is made up of this call and response.** As we sing together, we become of one mind, with each other and with the Lord.

6. **The Holy Spirit brings us here before all these other people and holds this community together, making it the body and voice of Christ.** The Holy Spirit frees our voices and enables us to sing. He holds us together as a single worshiping body and so enables us to speak and sing together.

7. **In all Christian worship we declare that we have received mercy, and then we ask for more.** In all our worship we ask God to give us what is good, and to show us how to receive everything with thanks so that we are able to receive everything that comes from him as good.

8. **The Lord takes away sin.** He releases those who have become trapped by our sin. He has authority to act for them all, to release them from us and us from them. The Lord has the authority and

power to act on behalf of all creation and of each creature in it. It is his exercise of this authority that keeps creation open, so that it is not crushed by the weight of its own past.

9. **We receive this judgment and mercy with thanksgiving.** Our thanksgiving detoxifies and purifies us. This true worship enables damaged relationships to recover, love to continue, forgiveness to be given and received, conflict to be avoided, and new starts to be made.

10. **The Holy Spirit preserves the identity of Christ, revealing him to us so we may come to know him and see his glory, but not so we may know him utterly or gain control of him.** He gives us Christ, but slowly so we have time to become holy.

11. **Anyone who does not give his praise to God, does not flourish.** Driven by fear, we exalt ourselves, attempting to make ourselves master of those around us. When our mastery is thwarted, we are enraged and lash out. When we insist that we are above challenge, we are making a claim of absolute power, and so of divinity, over all others.

12. **In Christ, we may grow to be master of ourselves. We can take whatever curses and degradation the world throws at us** and reply with blessings.

13. **The passion of Christ shows us the unbreakable love and covenant of God for us.** For us God has made himself weak and given himself into our hands. A free and unforced relationship with God is open for us in the difficult and non-obvious way of the cross. We can take on this service of God to each other without loss of dignity and, in our worship, we affirm that true power requires no self-assertion.

14. **Christ is here by the Holy Spirit.** We are present to Christ, but the Holy Spirit hides Christ from us, while revealing him to us in the challenging form of the Christians whom he surrounds us with.

15. **The Spirit joins us to Christ, while he keeps Christ distinct from us.** The holiness of the head is not compromised by the body: his divinity is not weakened by our humanity or flesh. The Spirit holds Jesus out of our grasp and beyond the power of our perception. The incarnation of God with us is not a threat to, but a manifestation of, the glory of God.

16. **The church stands for mankind.** The church insists on the dignity of every person, engages with them in hope, pointing them to the promise of redemption. The society that does not hear the witness of the church is liable to subordinate humanity to other ends.

17. **In the church we meet one Christian after another.** As we receive them, and discover that it is Christ who is giving them to us, we learn who he is. Christ comes to us first in the form of these Christians whom we meet here in the church service.

18. **The whole people will be raised.** The church is the anticipation and the pledge of the resurrection. The unity of Son and Spirit, demonstrated by the resurrection, holds all these otherwise incompatible persons together in the love and communion that is the church. They mediate this resurrection to us, slowly, so that it may be internalized within us.

19. **In Christ alone we may grow to our full stature.** In him, each of us can become truly unique and individual, and be truly together with our fellows, and not alone. Every aspect of man can be brought together and integrated, not broken up or lost, so that man becomes an entire and coherent whole, a living being who has a future.

3

Many Churches

THE PEOPLE OF GOD meet as many different churches, scattered across every city and nation. Each develops its form of worship and witness in order to be Christ's body for the world in that place.

1. GATHERING—BAPTIZED INTO ONE BODY

The church is the love and truth of God opened to mankind. In this gathering, this communion of love makes itself present to us.

God calls the church into existence. The Lord says "Come." "So, they got up at once, and left their nets and followed him" (Matt 4:19–20). So, it must be with us. God sends us to be his witnesses. To be a Christian is to follow where Christ leads. With him at our head, we are on the way together with the whole Christian people. For the sake of our society, the church must be distinct from it.

Baptism

We enter the church in baptism. Since there is one baptism, Christians must regard one another as members of the one church, and so as fellow Christians.

Baptism is the start of life with Christ. As the baptism service puts it: "In joyful obedience to your Son, we baptize into his fellowship those who come to him in faith." In this event our conversion to Christ, and our rejection of every other god, is made public. In eagerness to communicate the radical change each of us undergoes, denominations emphasize its different aspects, so that baptism is sometimes a fraught issue. But we are not baptized into one church or denomination, but into Christ so we are members of the body that is universal.

There are two sorts of life: there is the simple creaturely form of life, which always comes to an end. And there is the unbroken life of God, held out to us in Christ, which never comes to an end. In baptism we die to one form of life and are born into another. We die to that form of life which is always dying, and we come alive within that life which lives permanently. In our creaturely life, death and life are two processes that go on side by side: we both grow and are running down and wearing out, and we will do so until we run out of life altogether. Life is pitted with death; when the holes in the fabric of our lives become unrepairable, our creaturely life is over. But in Christian baptism one life is being replaced by the other. The new life, immune to decay, is replacing the old life that has been ruined by death, so that though we wear out, we are always renewed and regenerated.

The Marks of the Church

Together with every other church in the world, we say the creed together. We say: "We believe in one, holy, catholic and apostolic church." The church has these four distinguishing features.

"One" means that Christ is indivisible and he makes us indivisibly one with him. His oneness and indivisibility become ours too. Since Christ is its head, the church is the body of Christ for the world, and Christ and church are one entity, the Whole Christ. "Holy" means that Christ is utterly distinct from all others, and he makes us distinct from each other. By "catholic" we mean that Christ is the universal who includes all creation. By "apostolic" we mean that the church has received the whole tradition of all the apostles and witnesses of Christ and it passes it on intact, leaving nothing out. These four features ensure that the church is the communion of the love that is true.

We say this creed together when we meet because it records the faithfulness of the early generations, whose heirs we want to be. They fended off all the ideological forces that would otherwise have bent Christian witness into pagan shapes, and replaced the truth with imitations of it. All such imitations are intended to deny the incarnation and reject the truth of God's dwelling with us. The intention of such a synthesis is always to justify the gods of the day and preserve the hierarchy in which the powerful are at the top and the powerless are at the bottom. By setting down unequivocally the truth in these stark terms, these Christian witnesses prevented pagan metaphysics from overwhelming the gospel and so they secured our salvation. If we realize this and say so, we will remain Christian.

Immersion as Our Participation in the Procession of Christ's People

Our immersion in the water of baptism is our dying to death and rising to eternal life. We say: "To follow Christ means dying to sin and rising to new life with him." Baptism is our passageway from one life to another. We go down into that water, and travel through it until we emerge from it on the other side. "Through water you led the children of Israel from slavery in Egypt to freedom in the promised land." Our course is set for this long transition from the life that is corrupted by death to Christ's unbroken life. Throughout our lives, we are passing through this water with Christ, making a crossing together with the whole convoy led by the Lord. With him, the rage of the sea will not overcome us, so we travel "in sure and certain hope of the resurrection." As one canticle from Isaiah puts it: "The Lord makes a way in the sea, a path in the mighty waters, 'I will make a way in the wilderness and rivers in the desert, to give drink to my chosen people'" (Isa 43:16–20). The Christian life is a rough passage. We have to make our way through a crowd that, made hostile by its own fears, sometimes does not want to let us through.

The Christian church is travelling through the world. We are on the move through our city and society, passing through every community, members of it yet distinct from it. The Lord leads his people through the world, on display to it, "in triumphal procession" (2 Cor 2:14). The column follows its Lord through the wilderness. "By day the Lord went ahead of them in a pillar of cloud to guide them on their way, and by night in a pillar of fire to give them light, so that they could travel by day or by night. Neither pillar of cloud by day nor the pillar of fire by night left its place in front of the people" (Exod 13:21–22). In the same way, we intend to keep the Lord in front of us.

Every Sunday we stop and celebrate an anticipation of the promised land. When the procession halts on the Sabbath, the body changes into camp mode. Experienced Christians take up their places in the line around the perimeter of the community. The hostile forces prowl around looking for a weak point. But by keeping their eyes on them, our watchmen keep those forces at bay and so guard the vulnerable. The community does not let itself become exposed by putting its least experienced members on the front line. When outside forces become explicitly hostile, each must defend those on either side of him in the line, "contending as one man" (Phil 1:27). So that the whole defence stays intact, they must not let the buffeting of the forces coming against them loosen their grasp on one another.

The church is always moving through a narrow defile, being pushed from both sides, attempting to hold its course. "The Israelites went through the sea on dry ground, with a wall of water on their right and their left" (Exod 14:29). The world jostling on either side may attempt to push our column off course, or attempt to haul individual Christians out of it. When the column does not hold together, individuals are tempted to wander away, fail to find their way back, and become "scattered across the desert" (1 Cor 10:5).

In our worship service too, we are on the move, as can be seen when we process up to the altar together to receive communion. As we go up, the whole congregation is moving, then standing, in a line. We understand that this procession of God's people stretches from our places of work and our homes, all the way to church and in church up to the altar. The resurrection of Christ has put us on our feet, and set us in motion through the world.

The Procession of Christ's People from One Gathering to Another

Each church gathers with other churches. We go out together to find other congregations of Christians; we ask them to share with us whatever insight their experience has given them, and we offer them whatever encouragement or warning they need. The promise that, "Where two or three are gathered together, there am I with them" (Matt 18:20), refers to congregations as much as it does to individual Christians. No individual group or congregation that remains out of touch with the rest of the church is likely to remain faithfully Christian in the long term. If it receives no orientation and correction from other churches, without realizing it, the spiritual and other pressures of the world will nudge it off course and its distinct Christian identity and witness will gradually be lost. We must seek both Christians who are like ourselves and those who are not, to see what insight, encouragement, or warning we can gain from them. To stay orthodox, we need to submit to the testing and challenge of the whole church.

The church gathers at annual festivals. Each summer sees Christians meet in their thousands, to celebrate and learn together from a program of speakers. These festivals are not new. From the seventeenth century, the Presbyterian churches in particular held eucharistic festivals, lasting two or three days, which took place every three months or so. Some of these became big tent revival meetings, or missions of evangelism and healing services. For teenagers there are holidays in camps in the countryside with sport during the day, and the gospel teaching in the evenings, perhaps outdoors around a fire. There are conferences, some academic, some aiming to teach aspects of ministry. And with all this there is the aura of celebrity that attaches to some speakers, musicians, and worship leaders, and a torrent of books, videos, and downloads. Such camps remind us that the Christian life is the pilgrim life, that we are on the way and so meet in the open air and in full view of the world.

At particular seasons, like Christmas and Easter, the church gathers out on the street and processes through the city together. In Advent we go carol singing and worship around a nativity scene in the center of town. The church is out on the street again in the season of Easter. We begin Lent on Ash Wednesday with a telltale dab of ash on our foreheads. In my part of the city, you can see processions on Palm Sunday and Good Friday. On Palm Sunday we process along our streets, singing hymns, to celebrate the Lord's entry into Jerusalem. On Good Friday we process around the stations of the cross, marked out on the walls of the church, either inside or out, to celebrate the passion. At the end of the six weeks of Easter we gather again at Pentecost with a festival. At Corpus Christi, Catholic churches take to the streets again. While onlookers are bemused, the police irritated, and traffic snarled up, we process through the city singing hymns that give thanks for the gift of Christ's body that is given to us in the eucharist.

The church also gathers in public for a range of other occasions. Whenever Parliament is considering legislation that seems to dishonor the life of the unborn and other vulnerable people, Christians in London hold vigils, pray, and process around Westminster. In the 1990s as many churches were working towards the cancellation of third-world debt, some in London started a "March for Jesus," which became an annual event to draw our attention to the Jubilee. Though some churches call them "prayer walking" or "prayer marches," they are the procession of Christ and his people.

The Salvation Army started in my part of London. These Christians adopted a particularly disciplined life because they saw how strongly despair and, with it, alcohol, drugs, gambling, and prostitution gripped society. They knew that only the disciplined and communal life allow Christians to withstand those pressures and help others withstand them too. The Salvation Army has stood on pavements, its bands played, have sung hymns, prayed, and celebrated the victory of Christ here for a hundred and fifty years. The forces of self-destruction still make themselves visible, and it is always obvious that some are losing the struggle, becoming victims of the cravings and dependencies that turn us in on ourselves. But by gathering to celebrate Christ's victory over all the addictions, hurts, and rancor, and by singing and praying as we walk on these streets, we demonstrate that God has not abandoned any one of us to hopelessness. As the church does so, it raises the hopes of the whole city and society. As the apostle Paul says, "We are the aroma of Christ to God among those who are being saved and among those who are perishing" (2 Cor 2:15). Though to some we may be the smell of death, to others we are the fragrance of life. These public processions and meetings are a fundamental part of the Christian life. All Christian life, and every event of worship, is a public act of witness to the watching world.

All the Generations of the Church

We are a people on the way: this movement can be seen in every Sunday service. You can also see this procession in more static form in church, where the more experienced lead and the newcomers follow them. We start at the back and move forward over the years. Other congregations take care to reverse this order, encouraging the new and young to worship at the front from the first, giving as many opportunities as they can to see, participate, and lead. As we sit in church there are people in the rows in front and behind us, just as there were Christians before us and will be Christians after us. As we look towards the altar, we are simultaneously looking at those who came before us, so looking into the past as it were, and we are looking forwards into the future. We can only identify this future by looking through all the generations of Christian history, to Jesus and the first disciples. By looking at the incarnation and subsequent ministry of the apostles, we can see glimpse the shape of the future, when all Jesus's people are finally united with him.

As we look down the church, we may hope to see in that crowd some of the Christians whose lives have impressed us. Some of us may look for Saint Peter and Saint Paul, for Saint Mary and Saint John; we may look for Saint Augustine or any of the saints and martyrs of the subsequent centuries of the church. We may look for Saint George, Saint Francis of Assisi, or Saint Patrick, and the saints of the Celtic Church. Some may wish to meet Hildegard of Bingen, Julian of Norwich, or Theresa of Avila. Some may look for Martin Luther, John Calvin, John Bunyan, and John Wesley. Some may hope to find the best-loved Christians of the nineteenth century, like Therese of Lisieux, or the Curé d'Ars, Jean-Baptiste-Marie Vianney, or of the twentieth, like Oscar Romero, Mother Theresa of Calcutta, and Pope John Paul II. Others may look for Karl Barth and Dietrich Bonhoeffer, Billy Graham, Lesslie Newbigin, or Martin Luther King.

These disciples are all ahead of us. They are only dead to us: they are not dead to God. They set out before us, and they have traveled further and waited longer than us. We can say, as our baptism service does, they fought "valiantly as a disciple of Christ against sin, the world and the devil," and they remained faithful to Christ to the end of their lives. The more experienced Christians ahead of us in this procession are here to serve us. They are only the best-known members of the communion of the Holy Spirit through whom good things come to us through those who are ahead of us. What they receive, they pass on to us. They are waiting for us and will not finish without us (Heb 11:39–40).

This communion of persons made holy very slowly mediates this holiness to us, so we can share in their fellowship and become holy too. They pass back to us the installments of holiness that we call sacraments, each of which is an intangible piece of the indivisible union of Christ with his people, and of the holy and indivisible union of God with mankind. An imperceptible stream of holiness is coming down to us, the resurrection seeping into the world through the ministry of these generations. The community that is slowly gathering around Christ, which we know as the church, is the first glimmerings of the resurrection. This is why at your baptism we pray: "May God who has received you by Baptism into his church, pour upon you the riches of his grace, that within the company of Christ's pilgrim people you may daily be renewed by his anointing Spirit and come into the inheritance of the saints in glory."

Rival Loves

The church is the people whom Christ gathers around himself. But there are many other assemblies and gatherings, not focused on Christ, but on other individuals or other movements. The world is made up of people swirling around, gathering around one movement or figure, and then moving on to the next. When the Christian community proclaims that the God of Jesus Christ is the only God, it does not say this in a vacuum. It says it in a world of voices all saying something about who we should be gathering around.

All human beings give themselves away. We have said that adoration seeps out of us, and this makes us utterly needy, and that, if we do not give ourselves to Christ, we give ourselves away to some other power. If we do this, we give these individuals more adoration than they can manage, and so make idols of them, and they accrue a power though they have no authority. Our whole consumer culture is a vast adoration service that interposes various substitute forms of love. The love industries push themselves between each man and woman, always setting before each the image of a more perfect woman or man. As such, a vast displacement activity keeps us from receiving the true love that comes from God.

All the voices that make up our consumer culture tell us who we are and what we should demand from one another. They are making claims to power too, since they suggest that we let them make decisions for us. The church must be able to put names to these and call them the idols of our age: they are images of good things that, disconnected from their source, have become distorted. Whenever it is in session its worship brings the Christian community into confrontation with all other gods. The Christian community speaks out to the world, warning both how powerful these delusions are, but also how powerless, illusory, and demeaning its gods are. Every Sunday morning the Christians meet together to tell the gods of their defeat. The gods are being taken out of us, so they are made less powerful and damaging by our regular public confession of Christ.

The Faithfulness of Christ

The worship service is a product of Christ's worship and service of God. But Christ also makes himself our servant and serves us. The service is two things, therefore. It is the Son's eternal conversation with the Father, and it is the Son's service to us. He works for us, and provides for us, and the church is the form of his service. This second meaning is the basis of the first. God creates this gathering of people and their worship for us. This worship starts before we arrive and continues after we have left. This service of the whole company around God goes on over our heads, and it spills over from heaven in the form of the events of worship that we know, so that what we experience in church is a relay from heaven.

The church service also generates Christian ministry. This worship powers the Christian mission to the world. Christians withhold worship from everyone who is not God, and so withhold excessive acknowledgment from all other authorities. Our worship of God debunks and demythologizes them, and this is our fundamental service to the world. The possibility of this true worship, and thus the possibility of truth, and the consequent denial of false worship, is our witness to God and our contribution to our society.

The church is public and visible, which means that it is also institutional. It is a generous thing to be available, so that anyone and everyone knows how to find us. Our buildings are visible, and opening hours are just as long as they can be. You do not have to make an appointment or join a queue. The church is a publicly available institution so that people know where to find us.

The church gathers in a particular place. We meet here on behalf of the whole people of London. London is my place, yours is somewhere else perhaps. When it gathers, the church intercedes for its own locality, speaking on its behalf to God. The church is good for the world only as long as it is true to the gospel and therefore is distinct from the world. The more Christians direct their attention to the society around them, and become nervous of how society will respond to the gospel, the less helpful to that community the church will be. Only by being true to the gospel can the church be of any use to society.

We are under a common discipline, and it is this that keeps us one people gathered from many. We are the church in London only as long as we are under the discipline of the whole worldwide church, and of the whole church of all centuries, from the beginning up until now. They insist so that we do not withhold any part of the gospel from London. Without this discipline would we become a clique of the like-minded and, in the long-term, just another club or sect. As long as we are connected to the other churches in London we remain under the discipline of the whole church. We will return to this issue in our last chapter.

2. HEARING—TRUTH AND JUDGMENT

The church that hears the word of God also passes it on to the world. It tells the world that there is an authoritative judge who can tell what is true and what is not. That God and no one else is this judge is good news.

The church reads Scripture in public. We read it, morning and evening, in every act of Christian worship. We do so in the hope that our society will hear the Scripture that we read out to it. When we admit that our predecessors in the Christian faith have been faithful, and have handed on to us the truth of Jesus Christ and his apostles, and on its behalf, we are ready to hear the truth of our society, and expect that our society will want to hear this truth for itself.

The word of God is heard in the whole breadth of Scripture. Since, for the sake of our society, the church must read all Scripture, it must read the Old Testament. We may not divide the Old Testament from the New, for so we will divide the indivisible testimony of God. If we were to demote or discard the Old Testament it would be because we did not understand that we are gentiles, the latecomers introduced into the long-existing community of God. This community is Israel, the people of the Old Testament, who looked forward to Christ and finally bore Christ for us. The work of God began before us and has created a community that precedes us. We may read the Scriptures because the many prophets and people of Israel have transmitted them to us. If we see the Old Testament as the testimony and testament of God, we can hope to join the people of God revealed to us there.

The people of Israel and every generation of the church are our guides and marshals on the path that we are taking together. The narrative of the way that the Christian people has to go unfolds through all the readings of the year, set out in our liturgical calendar. Each sermon helps us follow our own progress around the year, and so shows us that the whole church is together on pilgrimage.

Our identity in the narrative of Scripture and worship

Imagine you are in a place that you have never been in before, packed with people, watching a ceremony that is taking place in a language you do not understand. You are baffled by everything you see. Then, because he realizes how lost you feel, someone next to you in the crowd starts to tell you in your own language what you are witnessing. He points out the action going on above the assembled worshipers and whispers just enough explanation for you to pick up what is going on. This is what the sermon is. It is a commentary on the action going on all around us, in this worship, in the Scripture of the people of God, which is the plot of this worship, and in the world around us. This action is the entire action of Jesus Christ and his company in the creation and redemption of the world. Though this is most obvious in the book of Revelation, it is true of every part of Scripture. When Stephen, the first martyr, is brought to trial, he looks up, sees the heavens open, and simply describes what he sees there, which is a long view of the history of Israel (Acts 7:54–6). The action of God that is recorded for us by the people of Israel in the two books of the Old and New Testaments is going on live over our heads. It is reports of this action that we hear when the Bible is read to us, and the sermon is offered to help us to hear and see what is going on above and around us.

The good judge

When we are gathered together, we are in the presence of God. We say: The "Lord is here," and reply "His Spirit is with us." God sees us and knows us. He is the one whose good opinion we value, whose judgment we trust. His word comes to us as judgment. If he did not give us his judgment, he would be of no help to us.

In our worship, the Lord is present in judgment. As our judge, he now holds session for us. We are present in this assembly with all the rest of the world, and we can all see how things are. Nothing stays hidden, every secret is made known, and the whole truth is revealed. At last, the truth is there to see. At last, we can see that things are as the Lord describes them. His judgment will be ours too. It will be clear that the judgment he gives is the right and the only judgment, and the judgment that everybody concurs in and is pleased with. All who are present will declare themselves satisfied and glad. In Christian worship the ultimate judgment, the last word, is being given. This judgment is not fate, it is not cruel or arbitrary or unwished for: we look forward to it, we demand it, we protest when it is withheld, and it is a relief when it arrives.

Judgment is decision-making. By making decisions we gain the experience that will make our decisions good ones. Good judgment is good: only bad judgment is bad. If you see someone heading into danger, you shout a warning. You make a judgment, a decision, based on instinct and, if your judgment is right, perhaps you have saved a life. We act for one another and judge and make decisions on one another's behalf.

We are able to judge positively for one another. Then we can tell each other not to be afraid and not to harm one another. When we trust others to do the best for us, we can seek one another's opinion. Let us take a homely example. I present myself poorly. When you see how poor my posture is, how I hunch my shoulders, you demonstrably relax your shoulders, to show me that I am holding myself too tight. Each time you do this, you are enabling me to see how I look, and how way off my self-image is. Imagine that you see how badly dressed I am and decide to take me shopping for some new clothes. Each time I emerge from the changing room wearing some new item, you indicate with a slight nod or wince how suitable it is. Each of these is a little judgment. Because you do this gently, I welcome this rather than resent it. I rely on your judgment, and learn how to judge for myself, and so develop greater self-possession. We all seek judgment. The point is only to find the judge who is not needy and so has no designs of his own on you.

God is a judge and a good one. He presents himself before us in church to give us his judgment. It is because he is indeed our friend that God judges us and we have someone who can really tell us how we are doing. When we hear Scripture, we receive that scrutiny and examination, and we see how things lie with us. To conceal from one another the news that God is our judge is an unkind thing to do. When this news is not clearly expressed and welcomed, but ridiculed and belittled, everyone suffers. But when we ourselves are complicit in covering up the news of this true judge, that is a disaster. Getting the information about any public service is fundamental to that service itself. The news of God and our access to his name is essential to us. His true name is the means by which his service can be accessed. God is known not for his sake, but for yours. The glory of God, the extent of public knowledge of him, is not for him, but for us. To proclaim the name of God is to offer salvation.

The word of God comes to the word of mankind. The world is made up of the many words of God and of mankind. All our words are the words we are given by God, which we must someday return to God so that they may be renewed. For as long as they are not returned, the words of mankind will go round in circles and, as they become broken, cause increasing grief and chaos. Whenever this contrast between the word of God and the word of mankind is not made, the gospel is not understood as the merciful response of God to the desires and desperation of mankind.

The Christian account of the work of Christ, and of his atonement and sacrifice, becomes significant once we realize that the gospel comes into a world made up of many "gospels." The word of God confronts the claims we make. The gospel enables us to identify and diagnose all our half-truths. The worshiping community of the church therefore has to contrast the Christian message to all the other messages; it says that there are two liturgies. There is the Christian liturgy, which is true worship. And there are the many pagan liturgies, in which our worship is turned in the wrong direction. The first liturgy is directed by love of God to the perfecting of all God's creatures, while the others take us in all sorts of other directions, dissipating us until the truth of our identity is broken and lost.

Judgment and Mercy

In our worship we link this true judgment of God with our act of confession of sin and with his act of forgiveness and absolution. We understand what this judgment and mercy are through the passion and death of Jesus, and we are able to grasp these because we read the Old Testament. The church that reads the Old Testament is able to see Easter as Passover, and discover that this Passover is what now lies ahead of us.

The Old Testament is given to the church so that this holy community may find in it the means to read the New Testament and to receive it as gospel and good news. It will understand that these two testaments are not simply information about Christ, or about a timeless moral truth, but also about the pathway now open to us, and the power of the escort that will accompany us and ensure that we will complete this passage. The church that receives the Old and New Testaments together can see the promise of its rescue from darkness, the forgiveness of sins, and so it is enabled to marvel at its salvation and sing the praises of God. The church that does not read the Old Testament will understand the New

Testament only as an expression of timeless moral truth without any hope of forgiveness and transformation. That church will then be withholding that forgiveness, and leave its people in their sins. Then the witness and priestly office of the church to the world will be left unperformed and the world will see no salvation. For as long as this happens, the church is responsible to God for the misery of the world.

The word of God is heard in the entire prayer and worship of the congregation. Scripture forms all the acclamations, songs, and hymns that make up the service. All hymn books and song sheets are there to give us the words to sing, and our songs must refer to the narrative of what God has done. The aim is that the congregation come to know its hymns and songs for itself and so offer the narrative that gives our identity. These are the words found good by previous generations. Along with Scripture, we should learn the hymns and prayers of the church by heart. You need to know who you are. Only their songs and narratives will tell you who you are.

The church must pass on the word that it receives. The prayers and responses collected in "Common Worship," the service book of the Church of England, represents the repository entrusted to us for the sake of a new generation for the church in our society. Your church may have a similar form of published service, but even if it does not, it has an oral tradition, a regular way of doing things. We have to pass this worship on to future generations. As the witness and servant of God, the church is constantly watched and judged, for the Lord intends that we pass on the word that we have received. When the church does not do so, it sins against those for whom this word was entrusted to it, and since God has taken the side of these, it sins against God. Christians are therefore more under the scrutiny and judgment of God than anyone else.

Christians must also listen to the world, compassionately but critically. They do not have to accept its own account of its predicament. They are summoned to judge all the claims of the world. Only the church says that mankind is a mystery and a wonder, knowable yet never utterly known, who will always surprise us and about whom there is always more to learn. We cannot be truly known through the reductive concept of power that the world deals in. Only the church's language of truth, love, and service can point to the whole depth of God's relationship with us and to our dignity as God's beloved creature. It is this insistence on the depth of mankind and the world that makes the church essential to the functioning of civil society. We will come back to this in the next chapter.

In this liturgy we can speak directly to one another. We can charge one another with failing to live in peace and truth and, in the name of Christ, we can offer one another forgiveness and hope of reconciliation with one another.

3. SINGING—THE PEOPLE WHO BRING BLESSING

We are sent to the world to celebrate the goodness of God, and of the creation that he has given us. We are planted and established here, so we rejoice and are glad in a way that world can hear.

When we enter church, the building and the worshiping community, we enter the presence of God. Enthroned before us, he is "high and lifted up and his glory fills the temple" (Isa 6:1). The whole company of heaven stand around him. Each church service allows us to overhear as the Lord holds audience with all creation.

We recognize and acknowledge the presence of the Lord and of all his company. Some may bow or genuflect as they come into the building, some kneel and pray in silence until the service begins. Others simply greet their friends.

As it enters the presence of God the Christian community sings its thanks, with psalms and hymns. The psalms are the basis of Christian worship and praise. Every day we sing God's praise, and in our psalms and hymns we encourage one another to join us, singing, "O Come let us sing unto the Lord, let us heartily rejoice in the strength of our salvation" (Ps 95:1).

Blessing and Honor

God gives life to all creation and to all creatures. He names them, calls them and so they come into existence.

Words do not just name things; they also bring things into being. Words create life and can take it away again. People receive new strength from the words of recognition we give them. When the right words are withheld from us, our confidence and strength run out. Praise is the fundamental currency of human being.

We do not bless someone merely by making wishes, but by giving them the particular opportunity they need. In some specific way we grant them credit. We tell them that they can ring our friends and mention our name when they ask for help. We give them an interview, or a job, or a loan, or the use of our tools, or a place to live, or we recommend their work or introduce them to people with the same hopes, who could perhaps go into partnership with them. The blessing is not the wish alone, not merely the speech, but the speech-*act*, the decisive action. God blesses us by making possible what had not even been conceivable until he spoke.

We talk some people up, and we talk others down. We promote some; others we belittle, disparage, and vilify, and so all our speaking is either a blessing, or it is a cursing and damning. The world is a whirlwind of praise, in which we find respect and honor for some, and rightly or wrongly withhold it from others. As long as we honor people, giving them praise and gentle judgment in proportion, they flourish and their lives take their proper healthy course. When we withhold recognition from them, they decline, first in morale, then in mental and physical health, and then socially and economically. When, as a result of being made socially and politically invisible, without employment and all its social and financial rewards, they give up, turn their faces to the wall and are gone.

God sends his praise to his creature "When you send your Spirit, they are created and you renew the face of the earth. When you take away their breath, they die and return to the dust" (Ps 104:29–30). Christians acknowledge that we receive our true praise and affirmation from God, and we say so, sending our praise back to God. Prayer is "God's breath returning to him," as George Herbert put it.

We may not take the recognition or glory that comes our way and simply assume that we deserve it and that it is ours in an absolute sense. That "honor and glory" must be returned to its source. If we have done well, it is because we have been done well by. It is good for us to point out where all our happiness comes from. The origin of our worship is that God speaks in our praise. He gives us words of love and acknowledgment. He considers us worth it, attributes us with the "worth" from which the word "worship" derives. We direct this traffic of praise back to God, and say that it is God who esteems us and gives us our worth. Our praise of God is simply recognition that he is the source of all human value.

God loves and adores us; the more we give ourselves to him the more secure we become. We may adore him, but adoration sent in any other direction will corrupt us and whatever we praise. If we do not give our love to God, we will give it to those who can only become harmed by it. All human loves, even of parent and child, even of husband and wife, need to acknowledge their proper goal or their love will not stay healthy. The way to love someone truly is to recognize that that they are creatures of God: only this recognition keeps them and us safe.

In order to love truly, and to attribute worth where it is due, and so to regard everyone as creatures of God, we give adoration and worship back solely to God. If we do not, our lives become a search for substitutes and compensations for love. True love and perfect recognition come from God and are mediated to us by the Holy Spirit through all the persons of the church, the community he has made for the purpose. True love enables us to withdraw our worship from all other objects, and denounce our misdirected loves, mediated through the market and the various ideologies in the public square, and direct them back to him. This is why we want to be disciples. We see the point of instruction and are ready for discipline. The Christian who has been chastened by correction is able to offer correction. A true friend does not just tell us we want to hear but is able to bring us some gentle word of discipline. Not to give people the discipleship they need and want is as irresponsible as not teaching children how to manage their emotions. We need guidance and discipleship in order to find out how things work, and we need both to be told what to do and allowed to find out for ourselves. All the laws, guidelines, teachers, practices, and the exercises and books that make up the Christian life are gifts of the Spirit. Each has its place, prepares us for the next and each belongs to the whole package.

Christians are taught a self-controlled lifestyle, which involves turning away many choices, no matter how compelling they appear. When we do not acquire this self-control, we are shaped by whatever identities that the market is selling at the time.

According to the many cults now followed by those around us, we must be "modern." By this they mean that we should cut ourselves off from the intellectual, moral, and cultural traditions that have emerged from generations of Christian life. As a result, the assumption of universality that once characterized Western society is disappearing. All those traditions point to, and depend, on the incarnation of God with man, which is the supreme act by which God honors us. All mankind is honored by God. But other cults cannot acknowledge this. They fear that there is not enough blessing to go around. They insist that only a tiny elite perched atop a cultic hierarchy, can be worthy of honor. From the vast majority they withhold the blessing, and thus they curse; anyone who follows their teaching about cutting ourselves off from our source and so making ourselves "modern," is cursed as a result.

Each cult is about competing for honor and winning by beating and shaming your rivals. It teaches that life is conflict, fought in the idiom of honor and shame, in which you win by making your rivals feel that they are losers. The rulers of the present age want to trash our society and culture and demote us. Subtly they communicate to us a feeling of our own worthlessness. They teach us to feel useless, embarrassed, guilty, and ashamed. The lordless powers withhold from us the proper honor intended for us by God.

God blesses us, and we bless him. The term "bless" allows us to indicate this reciprocity, which is of course asymmetric. The term "worship" does not work in the same way. The Christian tradition has never said that God worships us, and to put it this way would be to invite confusion and outrage. Nonetheless this is the logic of the relationship between God and mankind, which God initiated and now sustains. God's "worship" of us is all that sustains us. God adores us, attributes worth to us, makes us worthy, and this "worship" that we receive from him is all the life we have. We have it, of course, only as long as we receive it, give thanks to him for it, and pass it on to those around us in proper proportion and so as blessing. And we return this worship to him, declaring before the world that he is the source of all life, and it is he who receives and accepts that life again from us, redeems, sanctifies, and judges it good. He is the source of value and so we value him; he is the source of all honor and esteem and so we honor him. This is the logic of the circulation of praise, thanksgiving, and worship that God sustains and which, within the body Christ, we participate in. The powers of the present age may withhold the honor and "worship" properly due to us. God, however, gives us the honor, "worship," and blessing that, in his sovereign judgment, he declares we are due. The powers talk us down, but God only talks us up.

Celebration and the Young Church

The Christian life witnesses to the coming together of age groups. Whilst we are in our teens, or students or young adults, we do not always keep the same time as the rest of the church. On the shorter cycle is the worship music of the young church. The young church meets on Saturday or Sunday night for worship and teaching. On the longer cycle are the annual festivals. The summer festivals are the way in which young Christians come together in worship, through youth movements, large-scale youth days, renewal and charismatic movements, and open-air masses. These festivals are not a recent phenomenon. In the eighteenth and nineteenth centuries, churches held vast church camps, "conferences" or "conventions," perhaps four times a year, with days of confession and preparation leading up to a communal celebration of the Lord's Supper. The church has always met and worshiped out of doors in large summer events related to the church calendar or harvest, with fairs and festivals.

The worship of the young church expresses yearning and desire. They express what all humankind feels but suppresses and is in denial about. Our hearts are restless, says Augustine, until they find their rest in God. There is a dignity in admitting that we are restless because we are not complete in ourselves. As long as we say that we yearn for what Christ wants us to have, we keep one step ahead of the love industries, which intend to trade on our desire, claiming to fill it but simply taking away all our means of self-control.

Old Songs and New

The church has many musical cultures, but most obviously there are traditional styles of worship and new styles. The church must always have both. Let us look at the new worship songs. We sing sets of songs, one after another, uninterruptedly in a time of worship. Song by song, we progress through rooms of the palace into ever-closer presence of the Lord and intimacy with him. We might say that some songs are too repetitive, or too focused on the experience of the individual Christian. But there are psalms that are equally heavy on repetition, and focused on the fear and hope, and joy and love, of the individual. We might say that not very much goes on in these songs, but perhaps that is how love affairs appear to those outside them. We are the bride promised to Christ. Christ loves us and gives us his praise, though in much of our worship we just tell him how great is our anticipation and our love for him.

The worship of the church is always both old and new. Through its relationship with all previous generations of Christians, the contemporary church is able to nurture the next generation. For this reason, we must look at the issue of what is old and what is new in our worship. If "worship songs" are new, hymns are old, so why do we continue to sing them?

Hymns have narrative. They give us the story of the gospel and teach us to place ourselves within this narrative so that we understand ourselves as the people of Christ. In these hymns their writers pass on to us something of our identity as the humble who are "lifted high." Many hymns and songs are interpretations of the psalms or canticles. The "Magnificat," the song that Mary sings when the birth of Jesus is foretold (Luke 1:46–55) is an example of a canticle that also has a hymn version. Every part of the Bible can be plundered for song material.

We have to learn our hymns and songs, by heart, so we will be able to sing them whenever we are far away from one another or in trouble. As long as we sing the praises of God through it, no trouble will be fatal to us. These hymn-writers give us the words to sing when trouble comes, and that makes them our friends. Their rhymes help us remember, and that is why hymns come in verses with lines that rhyme.

Since spoken languages are always evolving, any version of a song is always slowly becoming old-fashioned. If we left our hymns unchanged, changes in the language will eventually make them difficult to understand. Many of our hymns have an air of Victorian sentimentality. But we can give them new life by replacing obscure phrases and untangling their syntax to show the sense of what we are singing. In our sermons we can point out the rationality of what we are singing and so make all our worship plain. We can also write contemporary versions of them, which is what the Victorians did, taking the songs they inherited and bringing them up to date.

We can translate psalms and hymns closely, or we can paraphrase them loosely. We can rewrite them in our own language so that what they said to earlier generations they now said to us. This does not mean that we should only sing the contemporary versions, but we should keep singing both the old hymn and the contemporary version. They often diverge enough to become separate songs, and often the earlier version preserves the richest theology.

Narrative and versification

Why did the earlier generations write songs in verse form? Why did they cramp the sense of the sentences in order to make lines rhyme? They did so because we also sing God's praises when we are not in church, but in the week when we are doing something else. At all earlier periods, when Christians did manual work and traveled on foot, they sang as they did so. The first and most natural rhythm is the unhurried rhythm of walking, and songs with rhythm help you work or travel. A good song helps a company to go a long way, so the songs with the strongest narrative, images, and rhythm are best for singing on the road and survive the longest.

We can try to reinterpret songs, keeping the rhythm and versification, or even putting new songs into better versification. We need to do this so we can sing it with all our minds as well as all our hearts. It is possible to sing these hymns without noticing what we are singing, or even being able to make much sense of it when we do notice. But let us at least begin to notice. Our Victorian hymn writers rediscovered some of the treasures of the early church. Here is a hymn by Fulbert of Chartres (960–1028), in the version by John Mason Neale:

> Ye choirs of new Jerusalem,
> to sweet new strains attune your theme;
> the while we keep, from care released,
> with sober joy our Paschal feast:
>
> When Christ, unconquer'd lion, first
> the dragon's chains by rising burst:
> and while with living voice he cries,
> the dead of other ages rise.
>
> Engorged in former years, their prey
> must death and hell restore to-day:
> and many a captive soul, set free,
> with Jesus leaves captivity.
> (Ye Choirs of New Jerusalem, Fulbert)

Fulbert tells the saints in heaven to sing and celebrate the triumph of the resurrection on this Easter day. He sets out the reasons for his joy by giving us a narrative: Christ has broken the bonds of death, and is now leading his people out of death's captivity. He has won us back. We need to recover this long-neglected narrative that tells us that Christ has considered us worth fighting for, and has fought for us and won us. We do this by singing about this battle and victory. We will come back to this in our final chapter. If we sing these songs and make their sense clear, we will have joined Fulbert and those choirs of new Jerusalem.

The Christian pilgrimage can be a long trudge. We will persevere if we sing the songs that keep us going us, in step, and that give us the narrative that tells us where, why, and to whom we are walking, why we are doing so together, and why we are journeying through a world that does not like to see us do so. We can sing:

> O Jesus I have promised to serve thee to the end
> Be thou ever near me, my master and my friend
> I shall not fear the battle if thou art by my side
> Nor wander from the pathway if thou wilt be my guide.
> (John Bunyan, "He Who Would Valiant Be")

Spiritual and Reasonable Worship

The Lord is the Spirit. The Spirit makes a great company, the train that follows the Son and that is his glory. Jesus no longer travels alone but with all the prophets and servants of Israel behind him, and with the church that follows them. This company cannot be divided or broken up, because the Holy Spirit holds it together as a "spiritual body," a unit that cannot be dissolved by any other force, and so is no longer subject to decay. His people worship him in Spirit, for the Spirit who raised Christ from us will also raise us to him. Christ's resurrection is promise and warning of our own future resurrection. Our new freedom is the demonstration of the resurrection, which is making us indivisible, and has put its indelible mark on us, sealing us for a future with him. We are that community that knows itself to have been brought together by the resurrection that has overcome the power that set each creature against all others.

In the same way, the Spirit draws this company into ecstatic praise of Christ. We confess that it is the Spirit who is doing all the work in this worship and that he enables us to relay what we hear. We do not know, or comprehend, or control Christ or his worship, but we repeat this worship in song so the world can hear. These many people sing in unison, so they are alternately individual choirs and then combining into a single chorus. This singing strengthens our own self-control and enables us to subordinate ourselves to one another. The whole congregation is at work in this worship, for we take it in turns to speak and to listen, or to sing and to listen. Groups of singers alternate and then speak or sing in chorus. Every part of the service is antiphonal.

Singing "with your heart" means with the whole person, body and mind. Speaking is reasoning, "with your mind" (1 Cor 14:15). This is our "spiritual worship" (Rom 12:1). Paul's term (*logike latreia*) can also be read as "logical" or "rational," by which he means that our worship is not just a series of musical sounds but is expressed in words and sentences, for it intends to be public speech, comprehensible to anyone who hears it (1 Cor 14:16).

The worshiping church alternates between singing on one hand and speaking and listening on the other. When we sing, we are acting as whole, spiritual persons. When we speak and listen, we act as minds that reason with other created minds. Reasoning, mind to mind, enables us to participate in the singing, in which we communicate with our society as a whole. Everything that the church does "must be done for the strengthening of the Church," the apostle Paul says (1 Cor 14:26). The same Spirit who brings about this harmony of voices also makes us a speaking, hearing, and reasoning people. In us, earth listens to heaven, then sings back, then listens again, then joins in with heaven.

Only the people of the resurrection can suffer and experience the passion, and become intercessors for the world, and respond to this promise of redemption with thanksgiving. Prayer therefore has to be taught and learned. Our worship sets out patterns which set out an alternation between prayer leader and people. This alternation or antiphony indicates that each member of the body listens to all other members, and acknowledges them as equals, "members of one body" (Eph 4:25). He gives pauses in which we put our own prayers for the particular people and situations that concern us. They introduce their prayers, and then gather them in a prayer (the "collect") that collects and summarizes all our prayers. This prayer must refer to the Scripture we have heard and all the other people we have prayed for. Once again, we have a conversation. As we learn this pattern, we know when it is our turn. For this reason, we have no reason to insist that all prayer is made on the moment, without preparation. We follow the forms given to us, and the whole service teaches us how to sing and speak and pray.

This participation in the service of the Spirit makes us free. He brings us to Christ and so releases us from every other master and enables us to confess no lord but this one. Now that we have identified the Lord, the right Lord, we can be fearless in the face of other masters. We are no longer tongue-tied, humiliated, and silent, but are becoming an articulate people. Whenever it is in session, the Christian community speaks out to the world, telling it how demeaning, and how powerless and illusory, its gods are.

4. PRAYING — CONFESSION AND RELEASE

The community that has received the promise of the resurrection is able to confess their sins and receive forgiveness and new life.

The Cross of Christ

We come in to church and stand facing the Lord. Ahead of us is an altar or table with a cross on it. Perhaps there is a cross depicted in the window above, and another cross leads the procession that brings us in and out of our assembly. The cross enables us to identify our Lord and orient ourselves towards him. We live under this cross. "He opened wide his arms for us." Arms outstretched, Christ covers us and give us shelter. He is the canopy of the covenant under which we have come.

Perhaps we wear a crucifix or sign ourselves with the sign of the cross. Each crucifix portrays the crucifixion of Christ. It looks as though he is alone on the cross. But Christ is only there *as us*. Mankind is the figure on that cross in pain and anguish. The cross shows us that Christ sees us and knows that this is what we are. We are the ones squirming in the grip of our passions and slowly consumed by them. We inflict this conflict on each other and on ourselves. We are on this cross, and in this misery, and heading for this death and hell.

But Christ does not leave us alone there. He remains among us, and stands with us. The figure on the cross is Christ and us together. We shut ourselves in a small and vicious place where we were sure that God could not reach us. But Christ has entered that place and become one of us. Christ has come to us who, in our distress and agony, are pulling ourselves apart. He has taken on our body and entered our mental and spiritual disintegration. He knows the place we are in, from inside. He has no reason to be here, with us; he could leave, but he remains. It is we who are inflicting this pain, on ourselves and also on him. We do not stop inflicting it and seem ready to destroy ourselves and him. But Christ stays here with us and withstands whatever we inflict. Finally, our ability to sustain this agony is broken. Mankind is exhausted by his own conflict and agony, and his power to inflict it is broken. Christ has withstood the power of mankind to impose this passion. Our ability to destroy ourselves is overcome by Christ's ability to withstand us and stop our career towards destruction. On this cross Christ has triumphed over everything that bound us.

> I bind this day to me for ever,
> by power of faith, Christ's Incarnation;
> his baptism in Jordan river;
> his death on cross for my salvation;
> his bursting from the spiced tomb;
> his riding up the heavenly way;
> his coming at the day of doom.
> (St Patrick's Breastplate)

Repentance and forgiveness

In the eucharistic prayers we hear that "God so loved the world that he gave his only Son Jesus Christ to save us from our sins."

Christ saves us from our sins. We may therefore confess our sins and be released from them. Sin is made of all our unfinished business, all that we cannot cope with. It is not initially serious, but it becomes so if it is left unidentified and untreated. The only treatment for sin is confession and repentance, that is, we may name it, drop it, and walk away from it.

We can repent. This is where the Christian faith is on its own. No other world-religion offers forgiveness. They can offer bravery in the face of fate, and they can offer ways to come to terms with oblivion. But the gospel brings the forgiveness of sins. We can let go of the past so we are not trapped in a cycle of revenge and retaliation. Forgiveness lifts us out a system that is closed. It gives us a future. The prayer of forgiveness is spoken over us: "Almighty God, who forgives all who truly repent, have mercy upon you, pardon and deliver you from all your sins, confirm and strengthen you in all goodness, and keep you in life eternal."

Each of us is curved in on ourselves. Sealed in our separate spheres we float past one another, me in flight from you and you from me. Each of us stands on our own planet, defending ourselves from the incursions from others, but utterly alone, while telling ourselves that this is not loneliness but independence. Christ bursts the bubble in which each of us is trapped and releases us. He unrolls us and stands us upright before one another. He gives you to me and me to you, and so brings us together.

By this absolution the church publicly authorizes and empowers me to let go of my sin and go free. The exchange of the peace is my release from the relationships I have not been able to sustain and my reconciliation with all those who have rightly laid charges against me. The church prays: "May Almighty God deliver you from the powers of darkness, restore in you the image of his glory and lead you in the light and obedience of Christ."

Confession

We can confess our sins. We do this together in the course of our worship service. We may also confess them individually before the service, and we will be taught the prayers that will carry us through such trials in the future. We can go to the priest and tell them whatever we like and so unload everything that we ourselves cannot deal with. In Orthodox churches you can see people making their confession as the service is getting underway, whilst the psalms of morning prayer are being sung. They kneel before the priest, who sits on a bench at the side of the church, and make their confession at his feet, with the priest's long stole drawn over their heads, concealing them from the congregation. The long stole of the priest represents the covenant of God by which we are all protected. As a result of this confession their sins are no longer their own, and they are ready to receive communion.

Confession may be shared. We carry one another's burdens. The real threat represented by sin is that it isolates us from others. The first step is to share it with other Christians to ensure that it does not have this effect. You are free to bear the sins of others, free to put up with the bafflement and misrepresentations. By sins, we do not of course mean simply fault and guilt, but the whole weight of promises not kept, expectations unmet, projections imposed, and all the unfinished business that we have created for ourselves or that other people have left us with and that has wrongly or rightly become our burden.

Healing and Release

We need praise. We are so needy that we give ourselves away in all sorts of directions in hope of it. We beg others to take notice of us. We spend our careers building our reputation and looking for whatever will make us stand out. We pray constantly, soundlessly to one another, and our prayer is a single plea—Look at me! We issue out a stream of demands and desires that reflect our neediness. Our entire career is premised on keeping this plea disguised and not letting our neediness become public. All the entertainment industry hears us and comes to our aid, translating our longings into demands that they can meet and, if we let them, they intercept the desires that should only be heard by God and so place themselves between us and God.

The church service identifies where we have been cheated of recognition and love. When such wounds remain unhealed, the original injury must be named. Maybe other Christians can help us reconstruct whether it was some particular member of the family or group who undermined our confidence or gave us some pervasive sense of hopelessness. They committed the sin, perhaps without any awareness at the time that this is what they were doing. But over the years we may have nurtured this offence, turning the original act against us into a charge that we hold against everyone else. We need the true recognition and praise that comes from Christ so that we can be freed from all these hurts and resentments. We may forgive those who have sinned against us, and so release them, and we must do this so that we are released too.

When we come into the assembly of the church, we are called back into our right mind. The worship of God punctures my excessive claims, and releases me from the misery of my self-hatred or my equally desperate self-promotion. The church service, which is the service of Christ to us, takes away from us all the substitutes that we place between one another and between ourselves and our Lord.

5. EUCHARIST—THE LIFE OF THE BODY

God draws us into communion with himself and, in this communion, we are brought into lasting encounter with one another. Christ has breached the prison wall that enclosed all humanity, and he has broken us out and is now taking us with him. "He put an end to death by dying for us." The Christian life is the long passage that we will follow through the whole course of lives in which we are passing over from mortality to eternal mortal life.

When we gather around him in the eucharist, Christ takes us through the opening he has made. In the eucharistic service this opening is denoted by the altar and the broken bread on it. On this side is narrow confinement, and on the other side is the whole infinite space of the communion of saints. But between this gateway and that eventual kingdom there is a long passage and a rough crossing.

Led by Christ we may travel into the unlimited territory of his communion. He has opened his body to create this passage that we and all humanity can travel through towards his kingdom, and all previous generations of the church line the route or accompany us along it.

The whole Christian life is a course of preparation that is punctuated by regular anticipations of arrival. We prepare by concentrating on what is ahead, and this concentration effects our whole routine and the place of food in it. We tend not to eat before the eucharist. We fast together: if you fast on your own, your fasting may separate you from your community, which is the opposite of what these preparations are for. Each Sunday and festival of the church year is an anticipation of that celebration.

The Spirit supplies the body

Christ gives us his life, and so we are revived and renewed. He is the source of the life of each one of us and of the whole body together. He dispenses himself to us slowly, waiting until we are ready to receive more from him.

Sacraments are installments of the presence of God. They come to us as elements of creation redeemed and made holy. The whole created world represents the provision Christ has made for us and is the tangible aspect of the service that he makes to us. He refreshes the world, so that it remains good for us, and brings us into closer and more lasting relationship with it.

These installments are sanctified, that is to say, dedicated to us by the Holy Spirit to do us good. We are thus being made real and present to one another in a way that will no longer be constrained by sin or death. As the Liturgy of St James proclaims,

> Lord of lords, in human vesture
> In the body and the blood;
> He will give to all the faithful
> His own self for heavenly food.
> (Gerard Moultrie, Liturgy of St James, "Let All Mortal Flesh Keep Silence")

We go up to the altar to receive the body and cup. They are given with the words: "The body of Christ, the blood of Christ." We reply with our "Amen." In this service and in this cup, we receive our Lord by receiving our presence from him. "By the power of the Holy Spirit, he took flesh." He makes himself present to us and he makes us truly present to one another. We are not yet truly present to one another; we are not yet real as Christ is real, not solid as he is solid. We have a sketchy existence, which requires us to be constantly renewed and filled out. But, supplied by him with his abundant life, we become more truly and constantly present to one another. Then, formed and transformed by the presence of Christ, we may appear before one another truly as representatives of Christ and so as servants of one another.

The sacraments are installments of reality. In that cup is the presence of Christ, gently portioned out so that, given time, we gain more presence from him and so are truly established. The eucharist provides us with installments of life that will give us this more true and permanent existence. With his body Christ is present in the eucharist, and within it each of us is being made more truly present. How is Christ present, and how we are becoming present?

Christ is present here *by the Holy Spirit*. The Holy Spirit brings us here before these people and holds them together to make it one holy body. The Holy Spirit holds Christ distinct from us, out of our grasp and beyond the powers of our perception, so he is hidden from us. And the Holy Spirit slowly reveals Christ to us, first in the persons of whom this community is made up.

Christ has come within the bounds that we inhabit. He has broken these limits and leads us out of them. But he also waits until each of us decides that we will follow. We have to *want* to be free of death, and so it is for us to ask him to lead us out. The Holy Spirit allows us to call Christ, and willingly to receive him and be transformed by him as he comes. This takes time, and all the time in the world is given for this purpose. Because Christ holds out this life and gives us all the time we need to receive this life from him, it is not a unilateral imposition. We gain our identity as we accept it from him willingly. He is able to outlast the resistance that each of us puts up to one another and to Christ. He waits for us to consent to receive Christ, freely. For this reason, he does not yet allow Christ to become visibly present to us.

Christ extends his presence to his gathered people, so that they gain from him their lasting presence. The people gathered at the eucharist are with Christ and are on the way to Christ. The body is becoming present, but is not yet present in the way that it will be. There is an absence as well as presence, so we have to look forward to, and yearn for, he who is not yet here.

The Holy Spirit places us before Christ, yet for our sake keeps Christ just beyond our reach. We cannot command him to be visible to us. The Holy Spirit himself remains anonymous and leaves no trace of himself. He is here to give us what we need and take away whatever we cannot cope with. Having prepared the place for us, he withdraws just as we enter, like a good servant, so that it may be entirely ours. For our sake the Spirit subordinates himself to every other person, making it possible for us to receive them without coercion and so in complete freedom.

Waiting for the Whole Body to Arrive

We declare that "We who are many, are one body, because we all share the one bread" (1 Cor 10:17). But Christ is not yet all in all, his body is not complete, so we must wait for the last and least to come in. We admit that "We look for his coming again in glory." Our account of his presence with us must include an account of his present *absence* and the present absence of his people. We acknowledge the continued waiting and suffering of the body of Christ and our imperfect communion. In our intercessions we name those for whom we are waiting, or from whom we are divided. We discern the body of Christ correctly when every member of the body is present, or is named in our intercessions. "Anyone who eats or drinks without recognizing the body of the Lord eats and drinks judgment on himself" (1 Cor 11:29).

In our own church this means waiting for those who are not present, and not beginning to celebrate until they arrive. When they do not arrive, the church sends someone to find this particular Christian and bring him back. The community may not start celebrating the feast without the last member brought to safety within the body. To start before the last arrives would suggest that this member is of no significance to us and not really a part of the body. But we cannot be the body without him; every last member must be brought in before the body is whole and present. The body that eats before this moment is gulping down only division, weakness, and ultimately condemnation.

Embodied Persons

We are persons, made up of soul and body. Our bodies make us available to one another. Without them, how could we find one another? Yet because we are also more than bodies, we are not entirely controllable and definable by each other. In all its particularity, each body is a gift given by God for the benefit of the rest of us.

Our bodies are made up of material elements taken from creation. They are built of all the things that we have eaten, the crops and the meat of the animals that have themselves been nourished by vegetation. This animal and vegetable matter, taken from the soil and transformed by the inputs of sunlight and water, makes up the tissue of our own bodies. Harvest festival is the most obvious celebration of our materiality and place in creation. All creation is summed up in mankind, who is witness to, and his own body is evidence of, this complex of relationships. Each human body is a miniature version of the world. As we stand before one another, and in particular as we are gathered in the eucharist, each of us is a microcosm of creation.

Imagine we brought to each celebration of the eucharist some tokens of whatever we are engaged in during the week. Orthodox Christians bring bread to the eucharist, along with the names of those they want included in the intercessions: some of this is blessed and sanctified, while the rest is distributed to the hungry congregation as the eucharist ends. The sanctified food we brought with us is taken home again to be shared with whoever did not come to the service, the old, sick, and otherwise absent, and eaten during the week. But the harvest is only secondarily the crops we bring in from the fields at end of summer. It is the whole of mankind that is the harvest of God, and that means clearly those who have not yet received the good things of creation.

Christ's people embody creation. Each of the bodies that make us visible and present to one another, constituted of all the plant and animal bodies we consume, is a gathering of the material elements of creation. Each of us embodies a particular part of the earth, so creation exists within the body, or as the body, of each member of Christ's assembly. Creation lives in and through us, just as much as we live in it.

In Christ, we are the "person" of creation, the indivisible unity that preserves creation immune from time and death. In the eucharist, material creation is able to sing the praises of God and so participate through us in the freedom of God. Since Christ clothes himself with his people, in him all persons and all material creation are forever present with God. In his liturgy to God and service to mankind, Christ unites all creation with God.

This work of bringing these many into one is what is going on in the great eucharistic prayer of offering, the *anaphora*. For the benefit of world, the saints who are assembled before Christ participate publicly in his office of raising and embodying the world to God. As Christ and his body speak for it and present it to God, creation's divisions disappear, there is reconciliation between the social and the natural worlds, and so we are able to live with, rather than against, the order of creation. As the eucharist is the reconciliation of mind and body, intellect and materiality, so the church is the union of humanity and nature, and it is freedom come to creation.

The kingdom of God makes itself present to us now, in a hidden way, in the eucharist. In the Spirit, the many people of his kingdom make themselves present to us now in this eucharist and worship. The eucharist gives us this thumbprint view of Christ, *Mankind-with-God*. The composite figure of priest, altar, and bread and cup are the viewfinder through which we look in order to see this view. The altar is the throne where God is always available for us. Flanked by deacons and servers, the priest is an image of mankind glorified by God. The bread and wine identify for us Christ together with his redeemed body, in which mankind and creation have their consummation. They can identify him because they already are what they point to. Christ has adopted and integrated this bread and wine into his body so, ahead of all other creatures, they already participate in the presence that Christ will share with mankind and all creation. We see God *with us*, and so we can see one another with God. We can see the future, and we can decide that we do indeed want this to be our future.

"Unless you eat the flesh . . ."

"Unless you eat the flesh of the Son of Man and drink his blood you have no life in you . . . whoever eats my flesh and drinks my blood has eternal life" (John 6:53–54). Here is a hard saying that has caused many to give up. We seem to be faced by a great puzzle. What does Christ mean?

Twenty-first-century Christians have received an oddly fractured account of the eucharist. It is as if the surface on which the plain sense of the eucharist has been written has become folded over on itself. Few seem to notice these stuck-together folds and assume that the surface presently visible to them shows all there is to read there. But they are looking at fragments of the message that continues, out of sight, on the underside. These folds have to be prised apart and wholly laid out flat before so we can see the message in its entirety. We have to spell out these cryptic abbreviations, and we do this by laying out all Scripture, all of which presents Christ to us. The eucharist is the long event of our becoming present to him, of his becoming visible and graspable to us, and of our reception of all persons as his holy gifts to us. In each eucharistic encounter, every event of gathering and worship, he draws us into an embodiedness of increasing glory and greater duration. He fits us for the consummation of all things, and so for reality.

What is missing in the truncated and half-obscured account is *life* and a way of looking that understands that this life *lives* and cannot be grasped by any conceptuality that can only discern what is lifeless. This life is this *person*, who is mystery, which means that he both conceals and reveals himself as the process of our sanctification requires. He is in charge of his own appearing: this is simply what we mean when we call him Lord and *our* Lord. The living person shares his life with all creatures, and the extent to which they receive and give thanks to him for the life he gives them is the extent to which they live, endure, and flourish. To ask whether or how Christ is present is to miss the point: the concept of presence is part of the abbreviation that has to be spelled out at length. The only presence any creature has is the presence Christ gives it, and this presence is never inert, but is the availability of that creature to other creatures, the particular way in which they are gifted to one another by their Creator. We will come back to this hard saying, "Unless you eat the flesh of the Son of Man," in the final chapter.

6. WHOLE PEOPLE—THE PEOPLE OF THE RESURRECTION

The church is the promise of the resurrection, and it is our evidence that the power of death has been overcome. Christ holds his community together so that it endures forever. The Holy Spirit brings the foretaste of the resurrection to us so we can now participate in this future kingdom in the church. For us the city of God is arriving, and at the same time it is becoming clear that, under all the appearances, it was here all the time; we were the only ones who did not know. God formed this city, that is, this society of ours, "for his own abode," in other words, to dwell here with us. This is his place for us and for him together.

Christ's love for us is the same love that he shares with the Father, so that this love, which comes from him to us, is the love of God who made all that exists. So, however puzzling this may appear, whatever exists is desired and is good. We can spend our lives discovering how creation is to be valued and other people are to be cherished, and despite all horrors we should not try to flee from them or discard any part of it. The Lord intends that we love, and love each other, and that means that we do so freely. Our love and freedom are just as fundamental as our existence.

The gatherings of the church are our evidence that Christ is drawing all humanity to himself. As the baptism service says: "Faith is gift of God to his people. In baptism the Lord is adding to our number those whom he is calling."

The resurrection is the demonstration that the Spirit has united us to Christ and, in him, to one another. No created power, not even death, can tear Christ away from God, or tear us away from Christ, or oblige Christ to let go of us. The resurrection of Christ is promise and warning of our own future resurrection: the Spirit who raised him from us will also raise us to him. This resurrection is hidden within the present world, and the worship of the church is the place where we tumble upon this secret. But the church is all the evidence of this being drawn together we get. The church is made holy, distinct from the world, for it is both the promise of the resurrection and the sign that the resurrection is already underway. In worship we are brought together with all those who came before us and will come after us, and all those in other communities in other parts of this city and country.

Christ lends his identity and very being to the church. He considers it his own. He calls all humanity into reconciliation in this body so that no part is any longer at war with any other, and steadily and with inexhaustible patience he keeps up this call. Christ sustains his body so that it resists all contrary voices and remains unified, so that, together with him, these many people make this one indivisible unity, so that when we see the church, by faith we see him. The unity and order of this body can be seen in the way that its members order themselves to one another in love. Everyone is ordained to a place within this people, and so to a particular station and office in it. Each of us is served by those more experienced than ourselves, given (ordained) to serve those who are less experienced than we are. So, united to its head, the whole church is priestly. The one priest, Christ, joins us to himself to make us his body, so that the whole people together with their head are this priest who offers the life of God to the world.

This little gathering, the church, is all the evidence we get that Christ is drawing all humanity to himself. It is not thrust on us, though. The unity of Son and Spirit, evident in the resurrection, holds all these otherwise incompatible persons together in the love and communion that is the church. Within this communion we learn to see all humankind patiently, not only as we presently are but also as we may be. We learn to see people together with their future.

We are in the world and so surrounded by it. But in the church, we are also surrounded by those who are being sanctified. Christ is really giving us himself, but these people are the form in which, for now, he does so, for "whatever you did for the least of one of these brothers of mine, you did for me" (Matt 26:40). We have to hold on to all the other members of this company and not let the forces that pound away against us loosen our grip on one another. These people are being prepared so that they can accompany us and help us to recognize all persons as his. Jesus Christ is calling, gathering, ushering all humanity along towards the Father. He overcomes all rival masters to bring the whole human body together.

The Spirit and the Good Order of the Church

The distinctions incorporated and affirmed within the body of Christ are protected by offices within the church. The Lord sanctifies specific office-holders in the body in order to serve us and do us good. They ensure that we do not form into narrower, less tolerant groups; their discipline enables us to accept the ordering of the whole catholic body within which all differences may flourish. Just as the whole church is under the discipline given by Christ, each congregation is under the discipline of the whole church, worldwide and of all generations.

A church without leaders and disciplinarians is not a well-ordered church. Christians who do not receive this discipline and oversight will not flourish, just as children cannot flourish when they do not know where the boundaries are. The Christians who do not receive their shaping from the whole church always push a little further, each a step away from truth, nearer to heresy and closer to their collapse into a cult. The church has to understand that each episode of transgression is motivated by the desire to be more closely loved and more firmly guided. Each congregation pushes its leaders. If they do not push back and reprimand us, it is because they fear us too much and love us too little. Whenever we see our minister, we must remind him of what he has been given to say to the church.

Each church sends apostles to other churches and receives them from other churches. Every church is part of the whole church as it receives the teaching and discipline of these apostles from the rest of the church. This apostle therefore represents the whole church and not only the community or denomination we are comfortable with. We cannot turn away from other churches without shutting ourselves off from our own future in Christ's body. Every eucharist and every event of ecumenism is an event of judgment and repentance, and of forgiveness and reconciliation, in which we look forward to being reconciled with those from whom we are still separated. Every church must humbly offer its faith to every other, submit itself to the questioning of every other church, and attempt to learn from them all. The one church exists as each church gives and receives the instruction and oversight of every other. We will come back to this in our final last chapter.

The Holy Spirit who always accompanies Christ can make him visible or invisible to us. The Holy Spirit holds Christ distinct above us, out of our grasp. And the Holy Spirit brings us here before all these other people and holds this disparate and implausible community together, making it one body. The Holy Spirit hides Christ from us, and reveals him to us, bit by bit, in the persons of whom this community it made up. Christ is hidden here before our very eyes. Who Christ is dawns on us only as we realize the people standing around us in church are his. The people brought into this gathering appear entirely different from one another, for they represent the whole variety of humanity of every background and situation. We learn who Christ is as it becomes clear that all these different people are part of his entourage, his train and his glory. As more of them come into the gathering, we may realize that he brings together people from all corners of the world and reconciles people who would otherwise be irreconcilably different. Even those who take their identity from their hatred of one another and were enemies now sit next to each other.

Perhaps this great crowd of people is easier to see in an Orthodox church. At the front stands the "iconostasis," the large partition that is entirely covered with images of Christians of previous generations. These saints are clustered around Christ, or beneath him if his image is high up above us all, in the apse or dome where he is portrayed in glory, with all the members of his kingdom about him.

Priests and servers bow to one another because each recognizes the other as Christ's. We could bow before every other member of the congregation, since all are becoming translucent to Christ. "Greet one another with a holy embrace" (1 Cor 16:20), as Paul says, for in doing so you are greeting Christ. But for now, we let bowing to some serve for bowing before the whole body. We do not want this strangeness to get in your way. Many assemblies of Christians do not make use of these images or these vestments and do everything with as little ceremony as possible because they are determined that these should not become an obstacle. Nevertheless, these images and movements tell us that we are all becoming images of Christ that radiate his glory.

The church is the assembly of all the members of Christ, not only those who are alive with us now, but those of all times. In the church the saints are not behind us, in our past, but ahead of us, in our future. All these Christians look forward to the time when we take up our place with them. Though for us these Christians may be dead, vanished, and forgotten, no human being is so to Christ. He holds them in life, for nothing can remain dead or unhearing when he calls. In the body of Christ, we may stop running away from all previous generations, turn around and go back, and be reconciled to them. We may give up our betrayal of these witnesses, and our renunciation of this tradition and history, in order to be "modern" in any sense defined by the world and acceptable to it. We are cut off no longer; now we belong to them and they to us. It is these Christian witnesses only who hold out to us the truth of our identity. The resurrection that raises us to Christ will also raise us and bring us face to face with everyone. He now sends us all these people ahead of him to us, so our resurrection, imperceptibly underway since our baptism, consists in meeting these saints who already make up his glorious body. Our future consists in being joined to them, the present to the past. This assembly, which is future to us, makes itself present to us now, little by little, as the resurrection is continually delivered to us in every eucharist.

Chapter 3 in Summary

1. **God has made himself known to us. The Father of our Lord Jesus Christ is the true and only God.** Claims to absolute power made by, or on behalf of, other powers are false and destructive. It is the service of the church to say this to which ever society it is sent. Christian worship is this public service.

2. **A free and unforced relationship with God has opened for us in the difficult and unobvious way of the cross.** God has not overpowered us, for his power does not prevent him from being gentle, but his patience manifests his power.

3. **God judges us for good, and under his judgment we are brought towards the truth.** In order to help, we ask one another questions and suggest corrections.

4. There is one church into which we are baptized. **Churches must seek the judgment and correction of other churches in order to remain faithful.**

5. **Christians read Scripture as God's proclamation to the world.** We learn our identity through the worship of the assembly formed by the narrative of Scripture, and so by the witnesses of both testaments, Old and New, and by worship songs that are both old and new. We grow by learning the songs, prayers, and cumulative experience of all generations of the church.

6. **The church celebrates in public places on the festivals of the church, each of which sets out the descent and ascent of the Lord.** By celebrating the resurrection in public on each of the feasts of the church year we set before our society the question of its identity, its future, and its salvation.

7. **The church processes through the narrow defile of the world made fearful by the many cults and worships,** motivated by love that, without truth, has become idolatrous and destructive.

8. **As it celebrates the resurrection, the church is able to receive judgment.** The good news of the covenant is the basis on which we may receive the judgment and correction required for our redemption. The church has to identify them as both the judgment of society on

itself, and of the true judgment of God. When we realize this and repent, it is good news for the world.

9. **The Holy Spirit makes the people of God holy.** In installments he gives us gifts that will reproduce the character of Christ in us. In the church, love seeks permanence and so looks for the correction and discipleship that will make it permanent. When we exercise self-restraint, we can act generously and for other people. The church teaches self-control and the ability to wait. Christian discipleship sustains our self-giving permanently.

10. **The Holy Spirit enables us to acknowledge Christ and recognize what we have received.** He makes us articulate, able to sing, worship, and give thanks. Through him we are able to speak for ourselves and for others. The Christian assembly has the character of a parliament and court of law: its members may raise any issue, make any challenge, or speak for any community of persons as their advocate.

11. **The Holy Spirit preserves the identity of each person.** He reveals them to us so that we may come to know them in their dignity. He does not allow us to know them utterly or gain control of them. He gives them to us and safeguards them from us. We have to learn the hard discipline of taking these people as the very gift and appearance of Christ

12. **Our society believes it owes worship to many other gods.** It is not able to admit that it is captive to many cults; it refuses to name these cults or give an account of the religion it is committed to. By exalting himself over his peers, the individual submits himself to unacknowledged forces, making himself subject to their cults, and unreason proliferates until that society is exhausted by cognitive dissonances and distress.

13. **The love of God brings us to one another and makes us both human and social.** This love, defined by truth, binds each together so that it may be a functioning society.

14. **Those who have faith in the promise of God are ready to serve, take risks, and make themselves vulnerable.** The two fundamental motors of society, trust and risk-taking, originate in the culture formed by faith in the promises of God.

15. **The body of Christ is the presence of Jesus Christ to his people and the unity of this people with their Lord.** Individuals and community must undergo the long formation of the Holy Spirit that will make each of them mature enough to affirm the freedom and dignity of the other.

16. A Christian is a member of the communion of saints. Each may become a distinct and irreplaceable individual as they undergo a discipleship in the tradition of that communion. **Through this discipleship we may grow and learn to wait for one another and hope for one another.**

4

The Church and the City

1. GATHERING—PILGRIMS IN THE NATION

THE GATHERING OF THE people of God is an event of public judgment. The nation that receives this judgment will prosper.

The church is the unchanging presence around which the city gathers and on which society is founded. And the church constantly travels through the city as pilgrims and missioners to it.

The Christian People Serve the Nation to Whom They Are Sent

Christ leads, and his people follow. Together they travel through the city and the world in the procession referred to by the apostle Paul. "God always leads us in triumphal procession in Christ" (2 Cor 2:14) and "God has put us apostles on display at the end of the procession" (1 Cor 4:9). In the procession that follows the homecoming king of Israel, described by Ps 68:7–8, all creation is overawed: "O God, when you went forth before your people, when you marched through the wilderness, the earth shook at the presence of God." After the king, comes his army, his chariots and captives, and then singers and musicians, and his people, who come out to welcome him home. The letter to the Ephesians quotes from this psalm and then adds, "The one who descended is also the one who ascended higher than all the heavens, in order to fill the whole universe" (Eph 4:10). We are on the move behind our Lord, and though the world may not see him, they see us.

And the Christian people stand in the middle of the city and remain here, the one constant presence. The city swirls around them, and sometimes rages against them. Their Lord is the rock on which everything permanent is built, and against which each violent force crashes and destroys itself.

There have been Christians standing in my city, and processing publicly through it, since the first century. Clement of Rome tells us that Aristobulus, whose name is mentioned by Paul (Rom 16:10), ended his days as leader of the church in Britannia. Though records of the church in London disappeared during the Saxon pagan invasions, they resumed under Augustine of Canterbury in the sixth century. Christians have stood their ground here, sung here, and prayed for this city for the fourteen hundred years since then. The Christians walk and worship, and stand and sing, and the well-being of this city depends on it.

We travel in good company. Many Christians are given to us so that they can accompany us, in order that we may all be formed by the deep and wide witness of the church. The church gives us those Christians who have sufficient spiritual authority to lead us. Being under true authority is good for us and central to the gospel. Our Lord gives us specific leaders to train and disciple us. They, and the tradition and the discipline they introduce us to, are fundamental to our discipleship. The body of Christ is not a merely theoretical authority that we choose to receive if we want to. It comes to us as particular persons who have been given authority for our sake, and our sanctification depends on our learning what they have to teach us.

The Monks and the Abbey

A mile upstream from the city of London there is a church dedicated to St Peter. It was built by Benedictine monks as their abbey church. An abbey is the church of a monastery, a community of Christians who have withdrawn from the world to dedicate themselves to singing the praises of God. This worship has a long-term effect that is particularly easy to see in the case of this church, which we now know as Westminster Abbey.

The chief business of the Christians in a monastery is to sing the divine office and to read Scripture aloud so it can be publicly heard. They do this around the clock, seven times in every twenty-four hours. They are thoroughly immersed in the psalms, and so they are familiar with every motivation and emotion experienced and expressed there by the people of God. The psalms teach them how to be glad, and how to lament, how to yearn for justice and how to become the self-disciplined disciple who is content to wait for the Lord to provide that justice. From the psalms comes the self-discipline of the community that sings them.

From the disciplined Christian life of the monastic community of the abbey comes all the good practices of self-discipline and self-control. These Christians were considered trustworthy because, having conspicuously given up their own individual interests, they had no material stake in any dispute. Their way of life tells us that monks regard themselves as pilgrims here, and that theirs is a life *on the way*, and in this they make visible what is true of the church as a whole. These monks made good listeners. They were able to provide the mediation that could bring any dispute to a peaceful settlement. The forgiveness that is extended to us by God enables a new start for communities previously locked in conflict, so the community of the church that points to this forgiveness of God is good at enabling reconciliation. They found that they could trust the mediation of these monks because their advice led to a workable solution that allowed quarrels to be settled with dignity for both sides. They offered a way out of the cycle of revenge and retaliation in which the previously pagan society had been locked.

Singing that liturgy, which involves reading the Scriptures, and in particular chanting the psalms, gives this community of Christians their wisdom. As they became known for it, people come to this community for its advice. The community of the Abbey gave guidance, resolved disputes, and so dispensed justice for whomever came to them. This public service of offering arbitration and justice grew. The rulers of the people of this part of the country so valued the counsel of the monks that they built themselves a palace next to this abbey. They considered themselves protected by the holiness of that community, and in time, English kings learned to consider themselves servants of God.

The palace of these kings of England is still there. It is the Palace of Westminster, which we know as the Houses of Parliament, alongside which the neighboring palace of Whitehall later appeared. Over the centuries the court of these kings grew into the organized government of their kingdom. Around the abbey and its worship, all the apparatus of the united government developed, and so this society grew into a single nation.

A thousand years ago, the king who first recognized this community of Christians and rebuilt their abbey was Edward the Confessor. Edward was recognized by the church and the kingdom to have exercised the Christian confession in a way that held his kingdom together; his faith had made it possible for him to be a good ruler, able to offer justice and provide peace for the nation. His good rule, which prevented the country from tearing itself apart, was evidence of holiness, and so his sainthood was recognized.

Government Gathers around the Abbey

From the disciplined Christian life of the monastic community of the abbey comes all the good practices of self-discipline and self-restraint that makes the good judge who can bring reconciliation and unity. The monks knew that justice is fundamental, that it must be tempered by mercy and forgiveness, and that this requires interpretation and public explanation. Subsequent kings looked to Edward the Confessor as an example and even came to his tomb in the hope that he would intercede for them for forgiveness for such bloodshed. The kings who came after him wanted to be close to him, in life and in death, so they were buried near to him in the hope that his saintliness would protect them from anyone seeking revenge on them. Many of England's kings and queens were buried close to Edward's shrine.

The church sings: "Give the king your justice, O God. May all kings fall down before him, all nations give him service" (Ps 72:1). "King" refers to any ruler: that ours are elected does not make them any the less rulers. They all have to provide the kingdom with justice, in the course of which they have to make some hard decisions. In the days before humane imprisonment became possible, rulers put to death those who threatened the peace and unity of the kingdom. Kings were well aware that they had blood on their hands. But they knew that the decision was either to execute their opponents or, if they gave them a chance to create civil war, they would have the blood of the wider population on their hands.

The Fragile Unity of the Nation

Since any ruler wants to maintain his hold over every part of his kingdom and to raise revenue from it, he summons an assembly in which every part of the nation is represented: this is what a parliament is. Any kingdom is always made up of different communities, each of which may believe that they owe nothing to any other community. Every ruler knows that the kingdom is liable to start tearing itself apart into rival fiefdoms, that since civil conflict is a threat to everyone, the unity and survival of the nation is always at stake, and so the integrity of our common life must always be their aim.

When too much is said in public, tensions can be made worse. Political leaders know that, when opinion polarizes, civil strife may follow. They realize that if they do not moderate the language of their discussions when they come together, the pressures that are always there may become destructive. Each member of parliament learns that they have to act as a representative, not just of the region, party, or interest group who voted for them or sponsored them, but for the whole country. There must be a shared humility, which is why parliament starts its day with prayers, its members publicly acknowledging that they are under the authority of God.

Once a year the monarch comes to open Parliament. He leads a slow procession through the palace that ends with an ascent to his throne, the place from which he gives judgment, which he does by reading out a program of intended legislation. In this procession we are seeing an act of Christian worship. For the law courts too, the term begins with a service: twice a year high court judges go in procession, briefly visible to us as they cross the road between Abbey and Parliament.

The church is the institution that points to the source of the unity and peace that makes this a unified society and one nation. The abbey is the church withdrawing from the world to pray, while the cathedral is the church making itself publicly available to it. Because this nation, and (around this abbey) its rulers, have listened to the worshiping community and received its teaching about justice and forgiveness, our history has been a slow and erratic movement from tribalism and violence to unity and peace. But this unity and peace will only last as long as the nation receives this justice and forgiveness of God. If it is ready to take this discipline it will continue as a nation. If it does not receive this justice and forgiveness, it will not have that justice or forgiveness to pass on, and the result will be that its unity and peace will unravel and we will stumble back towards violence and tribalism until we are not a nation anymore.

The Church as Source of Public Service

Government is public service. We have government because some people dedicate themselves to our service. We recognize them and honor them for it and grant them authority to serve us. The government is not there to provide everything for us, but simply to clear away the impediments to our serving and providing for one another. All government is dedicated to preserving the wholeness and integrity of the kingdom and the conditions in which everyone of us can act in the public interest and so be citizens.

All government starts as our own individual self-government. Those who govern themselves well are able to help other people to do the same. We recognize that what they do well for themselves they can help others to learn. Our personal self-government makes it possible for us to help others.

One form of public service is more fundamental than any other. This is marriage. Two consenting persons enter a public covenant to serve one another, and to serve those who can only be born through their coming together in this way—their own children. The public commitment of a man and a woman to that mutual service that will bring into being a family is the one thing that brings a new generation into existence and so ensures the continuation of society. It is marriage and the family that provide this public service; government and the state cannot.

The creation of a new family, which starts as a private act of love, becomes the fundamental act that allows us to help people, even beyond our immediate family and neighborhood. It creates a widening circle that includes schools, clubs, charities, businesses, trade unions, and associations that promote education, art, nature, history and culture, sport, and the whole range of our common life. This unforced grass-roots activism creates a civil society. Over time the same voluntarily public service may develop into the longstanding political institutions of local councils and regional government. Central government is that particular form of public service that holds the ring for all these others. The many associations that make up civil society do not exist because government gives them permission to; government exists because our voluntary service that starts locally, extends outwards and brings a nation and national government into being. We give it permission to act in certain areas on our behalf.

A nation comes into being when some public-spirited people dedicate themselves to holding the ring for all these forms of public initiative, enterprise, and communal effort, and a body of custom and law emerges to enable this. Government exists in order to serve the continuation of society. It must do so by acknowledging the priority of family life, and the creation of a new generation, over all other considerations.

Government is simply there to see that this open public space should be maintained for the next generation. The government therefore safeguards the interests of future generations over the immediate demands of this present generation. The government stands as guardian of the long term. For this reason, government is always able to benefit from the counsel of the church, the community that expresses the voices of the communities of the past and the future and so has to represent the long term when other public voices are failing to do so.

The Public Witness of the Church

Good counsel comes from the community dedicated to the worship and service of God. To bring judgment is a generous and public-spirited thing to do. Parliament is an outworking of this readiness to seek good counsel and benefit from it. All representatives, magistrates, and civil servants are carrying out the office of bringing judgment and providing justice. The law and the institutional arrangements of which our welfare state consists represents case law, that is the accumulated experience and the decisions drawn from it by generations of political representatives. It is an act of public service to sit in counsel, or to be a representative: you can get things wrong, with momentous consequences for individuals, nation, and yourself. You might well want to know how your predecessors in previous generations dealt with this responsibility and with all the issues of blame and guilt that come with it. You might well want to be reminded that judgment is a divine office, and pray for God's aid in it.

The community of Westminster Abbey sings the worship of God. It says or sings the office and celebrates the eucharist publicly daily. The worshiping community that does so is no longer formally withdrawn from the world: they are not monks, but secular clergy, that say morning prayer and sing evensong with a choir. These disciplines are still fundamentally monastic. Each church in London says the same office every day, singing these same psalms and praying morning and evening prayer, and so interceding for our nation and its leaders. Westminster Abbey is accompanied in this by all the communities of Christians in London. The Roman Catholic Westminster Cathedral down the road, and Methodist Central Hall across the street, all the Christians in all churches in London and across the nation, pray that the good government of God will be learned and brought to us by all these public servants who make up our national government. The whole church leads the prayers of the nation for justice and good government.

Secularity and the City Outside Abbey and Cathedral

The church is not on Parliament square by an accident of history. Where the church is, civil society springs up. A healthy civil society appears where all the practices of self-government and public service that are practiced within the church appear. Civil society—the practices of counsel and access to justice—clustered around the church because they knew that they benefited from listening to the church and from the virtues that are developed by Christian discipleship. The institutions of government came because civil society wanted to widen access to this counsel and justice so that it was shared throughout the nation. The church is not simply the one-time, past source of central government but the ongoing source of the innumerable initiatives of which civil society is renewed and sustained. Where Christians find those who are uncared for, they care for them. When some part of the nation is neglected, or when our rulers suppress the truths that do not serve them, enduring their contempt, Christians speak out. The vilification Christians receive is a measure of how far its rulers have departed from the true interests of the nation. The church is no vast political power: in every age Christians have often made their contribution against great opposition.

The church stands in the center of the city. The world can gather around or rush past it. The bishop and his cathedral remind us that church stands fast, while the monks remind us that we are pilgrims on the way and that we have no permanent place here. The city of London stands around St Paul's Cathedral. Westminster Abbey, the church of Saint Peter, once stood outside the city. Now the center of the diocese of London is named "Two Cities," for the cities of London and of Westminster. As the church of St Paul looks across to the church of St Peter, the church in London looks to these two apostles Saint Paul and Saint Peter to help us. The church alternates between this permanent commitment to this place and this pilgrimage through it.

There is more than one city here. When St Augustine referred to "two cities," he was contrasting two societies. The heavenly society is embodied here in the community that we know as the church. And there is the other community that we simply call "society." The church is distinct from society, and society is distinct from the church. This is so even though members of the church are as much members of society as anyone else. Civil society and the secular sphere are distinct from the church, so the public square has its own independent dignity. The church insists that the public square has this independence because it insists that the judgment and conscience of each human being is fundamental. The church points to this distinction and difference, and it does so for society's sake. The church's clear statement of its own distinct and holy calling is its fundamental service to society. It is the vocation of the church to safeguard the secularity of the public square. The sort of secularization that opposes the contribution of the church to public life is not secular, but liable to become first ideological and then cultic, a concealed claim to absolute power and so itself a form of worship.

In this city are two rival liturgies. There is the true worship that is directed to God, and there are all other forms of adulation offered in every other direction. The church embodies the progress of the divine liturgy through the world, which is itself made up of many "liturgies." When we are on our way to or from church, we are not going from a religious event to a secular or non-religious one. The church represents one religion while the offices in the city offer another religion. The church is one religious community that is always traveling through another, the Christian community on pilgrimage through the city's many other loyalties and forms of worship.

2. HEARING—DISCIPLES

Each church listens to the whole church throughout the world. The church in our society is able to be a good and faithful witness to the extent that it receives and passes on the discipline of the worldwide church and its teaching through all generations.

Discipleship and Leadership

Each community of Christians receives its authority from the rest of the worldwide church. Because the church in this city is under the authority of the whole church, it is the presence of the whole catholic church to this city. The nation that receives the witness of this well-disciplined and catholic church will prosper.

Christ sends servants to his church and himself ministers to us through them. They are responsible to him for passing on to us the whole ministry of Christ. They must give us to whole gospel and so bring us into relationship with all Christ's witnesses. We therefore pray "for all bishops, presbyters and deacons, that they may hunger for truth and thirst after righteousness," as the Ordination service puts it. They must be trained in the full deposit of faith: for this reason, we need an educated, ordained clergy.

We hope that our ministers will pass on what they have received from Christ and enable us to receive it in full and thankfully. They hope that they will be the love and discipline of Christ for us. We have to help them to be good transmitters of the faith, and we may do so by encouraging them to instruct us, and by taking our complaints to them and to God when they fail to do so. According to the preamble of the Church of England Ordination Service:

> Priests are called to be servants and shepherds among the people to whom they are sent. . . . They are to be messengers, watchmen, and stewards of the Lord . . . they are to search for his children in the wilderness of this world's temptations and to guide them through its confusions so that they may be saved through Christ forever.[1]

The minister can only teach what he has learned and can only exercise authority when he himself has been well-discipled and remains properly under authority. The church he ministers to will grow only as his understanding of the gospel allows it to. If his knowledge of Christ and his saints is too small, he will be an obstacle to the growth of his congregation. Each minister therefore has to submit himself to, and be formed by, the faith of the whole church. He has to study and learn this faith constantly in order to pass on the whole teaching of the church to his people, and they must support him so he can explore the resources of the Christian tradition and bring them the riches he finds there. They must demand that he does so. He must teach us that discipline, self-control, and the cultivation of the virtues are indispensably good things. He can lead us towards the priestly life, and show us how to absorb the blows that the world inflicts from time to time on the church.

The Well-taught Body

The discipline of Christ is essential to the good news of the gospel. The gospel brings freedom because it disciplines our passions, releasing us from our resentments and bringing us under proper control. It teaches us to restrain our desires, so we can control ourselves. It teaches us to find our freedom, not in evading the constraints imposed on us by others, but by discovering that self-restraint revealed by Christian discipleship and enabled by the Holy Spirit. Our ordained ministers show us the way to freedom through mastering our desires. They are themselves under a monastic discipline; they wear the dark clothes of the monk, and a collar that represents that discipline. When we learn to control ourselves, we are purified, lightened, and relieved so that, through Christian discipline, we may discover true joy.

We may control *ourselves*: in more traditional language, the soul may govern the body. Christian theology has a high view of body and soul: it does not exalt one and downgrade the other. We are embodied, and therefore we are present and available to one another, and thus we are embodied *for one another's* sake. We may learn to be more than simply our own bodies and needs. We learn to hear the demands of others and so we learn self-control. To exercise self-restraint is not to act against ourselves, but simply to act for one another. Our bodies make us available to one another, but we are always whole persons. Our bodies are therefore essentially social. Love is never *merely bodily*, and no act of ours is solely "physical." All meaningful human action involves learning those disciplines that allow us to be truly available and present to one another and so to employ our bodies well in service to one another. It is Christian discipleship that makes it possible for us to be free for one another.

We may recover the disciplines that allow us to reserve our bodies for one another in marriage. We may encourage one another to marry and in that covenantal relationship to discover how to restrain ourselves in order to serve one another. We may assure one another that, as the Church of England marriage service puts it, "marriage is a gift of God in creation through which husband and wife may know the grace of God," and that in marriage a man and a woman may be united with one another "as Christ is united with his bride, the Church." The clergy must honor marriage and tell us that it is the way that a society may nurture its children and give them the confidence to be mature persons. We may not break the link between sex and the procreation of children, or between children and their own two parents, or between this generation and the next. Children have the right to be brought up by their own biological parents in the arrangement that gives public honor to that covenant and vocation. The clergy must say that marriage is entirely different from any other form of partnership, and that marriage is for the good of all society, even those who are not married themselves. They must tell us that it takes Christian discipleship and a faithful church to sustain a marriage, and that it is marriages that make for a flourishing society.

Without this teaching, our society divides into age groups, each of which only knows how to pursue desires that are not ultimately social. Our age-cohort divisions are magnified by the aesthetic and cultural distinctions created by popular culture and the entertainment industries. We are encouraged to remain in an extended adolescence that continues into our thirties and forties, tempted to see those older or younger than us as an obstacle to our happiness and never realize that, all through the sheer hard work of bringing them up, it is children who bring happiness. Without that realization, our children are encouraged into an early sexuality in which each individual has to prove themselves by treating their own body as a disposable instrument. But children can teach us that we cannot cling to the present but must direct ourselves to the future, and so to the challenging yet joyful work of bringing them up to responsibility and adulthood.

We must praise our clergy as champions of self-control and tell them that we model ourselves on them. Only those who are able to reign in their desires, remaining celibate and self controlled, can help us. They must show us how to fast in order to recover the joy of the feast. The church that can say "no" to its own appetites and desires and demonstrate a proper self-mastery is in a position to help the world. The society that sees Christian self-control and desires to emulate it will be stronger than the society without this example.

Neglecting the Church

Ministers of the church must regard the church as the body of Christ, and not neglect, but adore, the church. The cup is bitter when it is served by clergy who do not greet the church as the body of Christ. When Christ is not primarily identified with the gathered community, that community is disempowered and its identity withheld from it. Christ is not to be identified solely with the unchurched: identification of new groups of marginalized must not take our gaze away from the body that belongs to him.

We must receive the church in all its marred and ambiguous state. Our conviction that it is corrupt, hypocritical, or distorted by structures or power hollows out the church and leaves all its members vulnerable. The belief that the hierarchy of the church is an unnecessary imposition reaches up the hierarchy itself. But all the ministers and institutions of the church contribute to the unity of the whole church and so to protecting the most vulnerable. Disdain for the church is simply a failure to love those who for whom Christ died. Ministers of the church who do not acknowledge the church as the presence of Christ betray not only the church but the society to which the church is sent. The pain of our society is caused by our failure to witness to the forgiveness of God that creates the church that is the community of the forgiven.

The Church-neglected World

The world that receives no word from the church is in anguish. The church has been given the words by which it can describe the trouble that the world is caught up in. It has the gospel and the tradition of moral teaching that has unpacked the gospel to many generations. It must hear the word of the Lord. When it does so, it can identify how the difficulties experienced by the different generations are related, as when one age group feels neglected or threatened by another. Without the church and its teaching, the world is unable to recognize the pressures that are at work within it and there is no relief from that anguish.

It is the particular sin of the contemporary church to hand on just part of the gospel. It tells us that we are victims but withholds that other part that tells us that we are also perpetrators and aggressors. But the church falsifies the gospel and betrays the society to which it is sent when it tells people only that they have been unjustly treated and are victims. The church is faithful to God and to mankind when it tells us that we are not held back primarily by other people but by ourselves, that is, by our own sin.

Responsibility begins when we enter the covenant of marriage, become parents, and, motivated by concern for our own offspring, become engaged citizens. When we put off marriage, or understand marriage in terms of lifestyle choice rather than primarily as a covenant of service, our own maturity is delayed and so is the emotional and political development of society as a whole.

Here the church has to bring its gospel of hope. It can tell the young that they owe the debt of life to the old. It can tell them that the love industries are an idolization of youth and belligerence that have entrenched a generation in their own resentments and made it unprepared to serve. The church must say that these idolatrous love industries feed on our gnostic fear of our embodiedness and our disdain for our own body. Reconciliation of these age groups and generations, and recovery of an age-mixed community, is the hope that the gospel holds out.

The church can also bring the gospel of hope to us by telling us that the given difference between men and women is good. It must tell us not to denigrate our differences and that the equivalence agenda is a false idol. We sin when we do not allow ourselves to desire those who are truly, by the fundamental biological difference of sex, different from ourselves. We sin when we do not say that the difference between men and woman is good for women and for men. We sin when we do not say that marriage is distinct from every other relationship and do not insist that the family and domestic economy has its own dignity that must not be denigrated or reduced by ideological or financial pressures. If the church is silent on these issues, it stalls our society's repentance and reconciliation and holds a generation back. As long as the church does not offer judgment and the prospect of responsibility to this generation, it is complicit in the disintegration that our society is experiencing. The church must confess that, because it has offered a merely therapeutic gospel and withheld the truth of our responsibility, our society has hardened itself against the gospel account of the dignity of mankind and shunned those obligations to one another by which the contentment of society is maintained. The church that has kept silent is an accomplice in the pain and suffering of our society as it rends and divides itself, which is why we are seeing a new and terrible passion unfold.

Two Liturgies

There are two liturgies and two worships. There is the heavenly liturgy that can be heard in Christian worship, and there is the earthly and worldly liturgy, made up of all those other forms of worship that our society offers to its obsessions. We see this liturgy of this present world most easily in the media and entertainment industries. The images of ourselves it presents us with are innumerable, but all together they show us that we owe endless subservience to a multitude of gods, and yet each of us is ultimately on our own. The liturgy of the world divides us from each other and then breaks each of us into fragments. It offers a sacrifice, and it is us who are being divided and sacrificed here. Just as the church teaches that mankind has been given a unique dignity, so it must also insist that each of us is an indissolubly social being, whom God will allow no power to divide or destroy.

There are two loves. There is the love of God who is for us and is determined that we should all be brought into that peace and contentment that he has established for us in his company. And there is the "love" of those who have turned in on themselves and are determined to exert themselves against all others. This is the love expressed by the liturgy of the pagan sacrifice in which our society engaged. If we do not receive the love of God and hear the judgment of God we will certainly be possessed and dismembered by these other "loves," and the economic powers that retail them to us. The church must nourish itself on the word of God if it is to defend mankind and prevent this society from being consumed by these other forces.

A Rival Religion

For secular modern thought, our embodiedness is an entanglement and misfortune. It assumes that each of us is alone, a mind only incidentally attached to a body and obliged to interact with the world by it. It encourages us to resent the demands of other people and all the plurality and ambiguity of life.

The designers, image-makers, and brand managers are the clergy of a rival cult. They fear and adore other gods, chiefly the god of power and the god of love without definition. Each cult tells us what each of us may want to hear, which is that we are an individual who has to free himself from the demands of other people. This single untruth unites all cults. If

I desire to distinguish myself and to put myself ahead of other people, I take the bait that each cult offers. But the moment I take it, I am captured by that cult and become dependent, and the appetite for its service and tokens grows within me. The clergy of each cult tell me that I will become free as long as I keep buying the service that that cult claims to provide. The entertainment industries and the policymakers who advocate for a re-designed humanity present us with dishonest images of femininity and masculinity. When the church does not proclaim the gospel that de-mythologizes them, these cultic figures grow to become its idols and our society will worship them and consume itself in order to pursue them.

Evasion of the love of God, and failure to hear the word spoken to us, results in this whole vast engine of delusion and hopelessness. We are running away from the only one who is able to establish and affirm us, taking shelter with those who will devour us. The pagans live in a world that they identify as alien and threatening, and they see other people and their uncontrolled demands as the danger from which we must be saved. The salvation they offer is a salvation *from* lasting communion into all those fleeting forms of communion that bring lasting isolation. Then we are caught up in an imitation Passover and a grim reverse-salvation. The cult promoted by the entertainment exerts its power over us as long as we are in flight from the love of God. The church must say that these many secular liturgies are only parodies of the divine liturgy and that they must all give way to that true liturgy, which comes from the true love of God for us.

The Individual Alone in Despair

When the gospel is not offered in clear public voice, social and individual disintegration results. Many seem to think that, before anyone can inflict any damage on them, they would rather inflict this damage on themselves. Better to destroy yourself than be destroyed by others. Better to despair than listen to the impossible claim that there is hope and life. How appalling to have this hope and then to have it dashed, they fear. The costs of failure are devastating. How much better never to have had hopes raised in the first place, they believe.

Our society makes despair its safeguard against hope. This is why those who speak about God are ridiculed and vilified. We can describe this as nihilism and irrationality, but this is the way that has been trod by a whole intellectual tradition that has decided to find its consolation in despair. They no longer wish to be confronted by their condition. They want to turn their faces to the wall. "Lord, take my life from me, for it is better for me to die than to live," Jonah prayed. "Yes, I am angry enough to die" (Jonah 4:8–9). Our contemporaries and neighbors want to pull the blanket down over their heads and find oblivion. Perhaps some are not intending to give up their own lives but simply hoping that so many of us will give up and die that they can inherit the world. Some seem not to care if they achieve this oblivion by pulling down the whole edifice of human society, so that no one comes after us. They are sure that they are not loved and are determined to make themselves unlovable so that even God withdraws from them finally in horror. They are certain that they can outlast and break the love of God. They are mistaken.

When the church is silent in the public square two things happen. One is that confusion about our identity and doubt about the goodness of human life descend. We are so convinced that others will damage us that we do this damage to ourselves in order to prevent others from doing it to us. The other is that too much certainty about our identity descends, and we seek to grasp a more absolute power over our destiny by assuming power over others. We become tyrants who regard ourselves as the only real thing, and who are determined not to be interrupted and inconvenienced by anything or anyone. These are twin temptations, to take power or become resigned and let ourselves be carried along towards despair.

But God does not give up on us and withdraw. His covenant is irrevocable. Even if we attempted to destroy all creation, we cannot destroy the love that sustains all creation and every creature and relationship in it. We can do great harm to creation, to one another, and for subsequent generations, but there is no corner into which we can crawl and end our relationship with God. There is no place where evil will prevail.

Withdrawing and Waiting

At certain times of year, in particular at Lent, our most important season of preparation, the church withdraws from the world and keeps silent. We let the clamor of the world fade into the distance, and what comes in the silence is some realization of the vastness of the dignity and glory that God has for us, along with the vastness of the patience of God, and the long-suffering of Christ, a suffering that he shares with every member of his body.

All Christian people are in training. We withdraw in order to get distance between us and the demands of the world. We may take on some of the ascetic and monastic disciplines of the Christian life. When we have withdrawn from it, we can see better how the world inflicts all sorts of unnecessary requirements on us, and the Christian can then return with something prophetic and compassionate to tell their society. The point of this withdrawal is to return to it, better able to serve it by pointing your society to what it is missing.

Christians listen, compassionately but critically, to the world. The church that lives from the gospel is able to point out when the atmosphere becomes poisoned by unsustainable claims, and truth is not heard. We point out when the world is making exaggerated claims about its authority and attempting to overdetermine the lives of its people in ways detrimental to them. It is able to declare that some of the claims made are psychotic and totalitarian, that the public square is no longer secular but has become a world of idolatry and tyranny, driven by cults committed to concealing the truth and destroying many lives as they do so. The church that hears the word of God in Scripture will also truly hear the distress of the world and respond to it in judgment and mercy with the gospel. The whole church, and every Christian, is witness to life and truth. We lay down one sort of life in order to take up another and so, for the sake of our society, we are ready to become its witnesses and martyrs.

3. SINGING—THE CHURCH IN THE STREET

The church witnesses to the unchanging faithfulness of God. That this community can worship God is evidence that Christ has joined us to himself so that we can know and love the true God and so live in reality.

Blessing

Thanksgiving is the mode in which Christians address one another. We thank God for one another, and we express that thanks to one another. Christ is entirely able to give us the recognition we desire: he has enough love for us. As a result, the church is able to sing and tell the world that it is loved. The church blesses, and encourages and commends, passing on the blessing it has received.

Christians send their praise to God, and as long as we praise him, we serve the society to which we are sent. The church is the people called here to sing, fast, feast, mourn, and celebrate. If we speak the truths of the gospel publicly, our society can remain healthy. If we do not dispel falsehoods, they accumulate to choke our public life. We thank one another for each reprimand, accusation, lesson, and reminder. We are able to name what is not right and to repent, for ourselves and for others. We are able to give thanks to God, to receive what we have as blessings. We celebrate self-control and discipleship, we celebrate celibacy and singleness, and we celebrate marriage, and every other form of covenant and public service. On our definition, growth means growth in responsibility and maturity, as much as in material goods or services. Our national product is a confident society that is able to bless and say that it has been blessed.

The Way of the Cross, the Way of the Resurrection

In this city the church must do what it does for every city and society. It must worship God in public. So Christians sing, to God and to the society to which they have been sent, and every church goes out to meet together with other churches and give thanks and intercede for the nation with them. We go from our church to others, walking through the city and perhaps stopping at any number of other churches on the way. Central London is my home, so these are the streets I walk, and anyone is welcome to come with me.

Let us imagine that you and I agree to walk through my city together. We could walk from the Abbey to the Cathedral, from Westminster to St Paul's in the city. We could start by saying Morning Prayer at Westminster Abbey, then walk through the West End to St Paul's, and celebrate the eucharist there. As we go, we pray and sing, and every so often we stop and pray again. We could take the most direct route, or we could meander through every street and stop to sing and pray outside each church. As we go, we can give thanks and celebrate whatever is good and greet them all as promises of the resurrection. We could call our walk the "way of the resurrection." Before each church on the route, we could stop and give thanks, celebrating that God has come to us in Christ and opened to us all the possibility of communion and society. We can celebrate each church as the place in which the body is healed and made whole by Christ. We could pray or sing on the steps of each church or outside on the pavement; we could even do this on the site of any Christian or charitable foundation, celebrating whatever is good and pointing to whatever contribution that institution makes to our public life. In this way we could greet all London as the dwelling place of the Lord. We could sing: "Praise the Lord all you servants of the Lord, who minister by night in the house of the Lord. Lift up your hands in the sanctuary and praise the Lord" (Ps 134:1–2).

But when it would be more appropriate to pray and mourn, our walk would become a way of the cross. We could stop outside any institution that represents despair and the disintegration of that communion, and there we could lament whatever is destructive there. When we see London as a place of exile and desolation, we sing: "We sat down and wept when we remembered thee, O Zion" (Ps 137:1). On our walk, we could alternately mark stations of the cross, as we notice whatever is destructive, and stations of the resurrection, alternating stations of grief and of rejoicing. We could walk from Abbey to Cathedral and back again, singing and praying the songs of the church, which are the love songs of Christ for this city, and this would be a day well spent.

When St Benedict said "Let nothing come before the work of God," he was referring to the divine office, in which we give praise and thanks to God. This "work of God" is the foundation of all our work and endeavors in this city. These streets are our pilgrimage route, the way of the cross and way of the resurrection combined. We can process, alternately lamenting and giving thanks, publicly on feast days and quietly every day. As we travel through our city, and against its resistance, we are making our Passover passage. When the church takes this way of the cross and is constant in it, the same route will also be the passage way for the world by which the world can pass through into the communion of God. The church will be this passageway for the world and so its way of resurrection to salvation and life.

Other Cults, Other Mediators

It is not only the Christian community that sings its songs. Many other cults and liturgies fill this marketplace and public square. London is thick with adoration, all of it religious.

When you walk through these streets from Abbey to Cathedral, you pass the headquarters of the retail chains that have a shop in every high street in this country and many others. Though it is not Christian worship, there is prayer and singing going on, as the creative and marketing people work the spells that will draw in customers. Sound and light pour out of each shop, each window displaying some aspiration, magnified out of all proportion. Each outlet works to beguile and enchant us with the particular set of sensations they communicate, hoping that we will fall in love with the image of the body that they set before us.

Each shop is a shrine in which some part of our good humanity is amplified and offered for our worship. Each is promising to raise you out of the ordinary and make you one of the beautiful people, worthy of the worship of others. They play the songs by which they hope that you will fall in love, so they can intermediate your love affair. But the only love that they can mediate is love of yourself; their whole calling is to assist you with your own narcissism. Every business that tells us that their services will raise us above all others is making a cultic claim. Only the true church is the gathering of all, of the attractive and non-attractive together, so it alone is the inclusive, or as we say, the catholic, community.

The Disembodiment Industries

The procession of all God's people that goes through London passes the clubs and shops of the West End. The images in the shops show us man and woman in their perfection. The travel agent's window has images of perfectly formed and tanned bodies, draped by the pool, with blue skies of the lands of our fantasy. Happiness is not here on this street, but there, on that perfect beach, these images tell us, so fly from your drab normality here to that perfection there.

In the windows of the health club, tanned and glossed bodies are on display, while inside the perfect body is being sculpted and toned. There is the cosmetician who will offer you the surgery that will give you that more perfect body that, you hope, will take away the frustration and disappointment of failed relationships. They will enlarge this part of your body and reduce that, cutting and reshaping you until you are more attractive than the rest of us. You may present yourself there like the animal in a pagan sacrifice to undergo whatever humiliation is demanded by whichever gods—youth, beauty, celebrity—you worship.

The procession of Christ's body passes the nightclub in which the liturgy of the world plays loudest. The club is a slave market where, no pretense now, all line up, eyeing one another, each is selling themselves and is in the market to buy. They hope to grasp some other body for a few hours, then detach themselves and leave again without complications. They want that first minute of encounter, but want to reexperience it continually. They give away all other hopes of love in order to repeat and prolong the instantly gratifying collision of bodies. All are hunters and all game.

On this street is the "pregnancy advice center" that will remove the child you conceive and so terminate your hopes of discovering a permanent love. Here is the pharmacy that will provide the emergency contraception that will flush all your emotional integrity away and have your metabolism madly seesawing so years may pass before your body returns to normality again. Then you can get back to your place at the bar and show us how just how cool and hard, detached and untouchable you are. You will keep your secret, and those around you will pretend not to know.

The church goes through the streets singing to the city and telling every individual in the city that they are loved, by God and by all his people. They may despise our love, but it remains nonetheless. Any Londoner may hunt for love in these streets and after many years find that they are less able to sustain any relationship than they were at the beginning. But the church walks, and stands, and holds out the love of God here, telling the people of the city that they are loved and valued by God. Christians hear the word and promise of God, and in our public worship we relay it to whomever is ready to hear it.

Raising Credit and the City as Global Mediator

Our prayer walk from Abbey to Cathedral might take us away from the entertainment industries of the West End and towards the financial district of the City of London. Here it is just as thick with adoration, just as religious and just as narcissistic. In the finance houses are choirs singing their devotion to us and offering to dedicate themselves to us. Their love is not disinterested. They want to raise money for you. They are offering you credit. In the City of London, they can get you credit in circumstances that every other financial center would regard as hopeless. Here you will find the most creative financial minds at work to provide the instruments that will conceal your history, disguise your weakness, and give you a new financial identity so that you can continue to present yourself as creditworthy, find new investors, and raise new funds.

In these offices, fund managers offer their mediatorial services for every significant transaction all around the world. They are all trying to bring business here so that no one can make a deal anywhere without London. The city provides the most sophisticated financial services, able to provide the liquidity that keeps all other lenders solvent, able to refinance and bail out even the most bankrupt enterprise until it can find a new more gullible set of investors. London claims that for large financial transactions only the rules established and policed in London, involving the most rigorous, closely defined and up-to-the-minute financial protocols, are good enough. Only London can provide the credit that makes every transaction in the world possible. This is the song that the City of London sings.

The raising of credit is what is going on in the city. It is this service that sustains the global economy, that makes possible our increasing standard of living, that raises capital for new technology and exploration, that preserves wealth and keeps the very wealthy ahead, well out of the reach of the rest of us.

But these finance houses want, and need, something from us. Indeed, they need to source everything from us because they have no life of their own. In this market we buy in order to build ourselves up, and we sell in order to have the means to do so. We sell shares in ourselves, and we buy shares in one another. We are on sale here. Most of those bought and sold here will of course never have seen the marketplace of London themselves.

Everyone is offering credit, but they are able to do so because they are always able to find naïve or greedy people who, entrusting their savings to them, give them credit. Though some hold precious metals, land and other property, mines and oilfields, and any great number of assets, ultimately everyone has just credit, which holds good at this moment in time. There is no real way of storing value and securing yourself against the future. There is only credit, sustained by the hopes and fears of a vast number of economic actors around the world, whose loyalties may switch and whose confidence may evaporate in a moment. Because life is unpredictable, all financial wealth is volatile. The city can extend credit only because it has borrowed credit from a society in which people are willing to believe in one another, and so freely extend credit to one another, a society and culture in which confidence and trust are deep-rooted.

Pagan Sacrifice and the Dismemberment of Mankind

Though every bank and business in London is offering a service that relates to a particular vision of our humanity, no business is able to point truthfully to the whole vast mystery of mankind unless, however indirectly, it receives the discipline and shaping of Christ. If it cannot answer the questions put by the gospel, it cannot be a shrine to the whole truth of mankind but only reflect back to us some distorted aspects of our own present existence. Each of their services relies on our wish to isolate ourselves from others; each of them promises to keep you ahead of the crowd, and more secure and comfortable. Each is making the false claim that inclusiveness and universality are found there.

Here we are watching the stripping and crucifixion of mankind. This slow disintegration and dissolution is a pagan sacrifice happening all around us. All our vast world-building confidence is the attempt to distract us from this cannibalization and allow us to believe that it will not touch us personally.

The church on the pavement puts its question to the city. How shall all this be judged? When the whole market is up for appraisal, what value will be put on it? Can London perform any office of global mediation? Can it do so without acknowledging that it is also under the judgment of the world?

4. PRAYING — THE CHURCH LEADS OUR REPENTANCE

The church is that part of the world that prays truly. The church prays and speaks for the world, expressing to God its helplessness and misery. In doing so the church also addresses the world and appeals to it to receive the forgiveness held out to it by God.

Under the Cross

The church carries the cross through the streets of the city, an exclamation mark over everything that it passes. It invites people to judge themselves and to help one another to come to a better judgment. One day they will be examined by the whole assembly of heaven and earth, brought together by God, the true and just judge.

When we carry the cross through London, we put to it this question. What is it worth? What duration will any of these values have? The economy of London is simply the sum of our action, and what that sum is is the question we ask by setting the cross down here. We may examine ourselves. We may put our questions on behalf of the vast numbers who work in service industries of London and Britain, and on behalf of the much greater number worldwide whose labor has supported and increased the economy of London and paid for the lifestyle enjoyed in this country and in the West. Across the world populations of workers put to us the charge that they have invested a lifetime of labor without sufficient return. The church may put their question to this nation, its business community, and the finance houses of the City of London. We may put these questions now so that when judgment comes finally, we are ready to give an account of our stewardship.

Christ sings the songs of the poor, overlooked or despised by us, and he sings them against us, charging us with their neglect. We must hear these songs and sing them too, and so be transformed from the proud and autonomous man, too far away to hear and too busy to reply, into the poor and righteous man of the psalms' description. We have the privilege of singing penitent songs and of lamenting with those who lament. We have to mention in our prayers all those parts of the world that have withered as London has grown, and we must ask whether the globalization driven from London has been the cause of their destitution. Have they been consumed by this city?

The Church Leads the Repentance

The church puts its questions to the markets, to the government, and to the nation. By promoting one group of people have they not simply made another group of people invisible? To nourish one, have they not consumed some other? We cannot be surprised that the church is not universally popular, or that its own members look for ways to reduce the burden of odium they must carry. Christians are on public display: in Paul's words, "God has exhibited us apostles as last of all, as though sentenced to death, because we have become a spectacle to the world" (1 Cor 4:9).

The church of our generation must repent. It has not asked the questions that would have prepared our society to live well or give good account of itself. It has not clearly set the truth out before the world and told it about the generosity and justice of God. It has not laid out the possibility and inevitably of repentance and our need to seek forgiveness from one another and from God. It has not taught the world how to examine itself and weep.

We repent of being the church that has not passed on the whole Christ and so that has not interceded for those who it has made invisible, voiceless, defenseless. We have not interceded for those whose lives have been blighted by the processes that have made us wealthy.

Every Christian is intrinsically a representative who speaks for others rather than simply for himself. The world may ask us whether we have not spoken merely for ourselves and not for others, and the Christian community must hear this charge and examine itself. Sometimes this charge is correct, and the Christian community has acted simply as another sectional interest. Then the church has to hear this charge as prophecy and as the word and judgment of God. God may speak against the church that has not spoken for the world. The church that refuses to serve the world and pass on what it has received is responsible to God for the world that now bleeds.

We repent of being an unfaithful people, too afraid of the world to which we have been sent, to tell it what it needs to hear, and so have betrayed it. We repent of having withheld judgment and the message of the cross. We repent of having thought we were more righteous than those who came before us. We repent of having cut ourselves off from the generations of Christian witnesses that offer us a much vaster gospel than the near-mute gospel that we have offered to this generation. We repent for having substituted activism for worship, for having assumed that we are more inclusive, less judgmental, more tolerant than previous generations of Christians. We must drop at the altar our belief that we know better than the historic church. We have not passed on the whole gospel, and our society has been suffering as a result. We are responsible for their sins. This cup on the table is certainly bitter, for it contains the truth, judgment, and wrath that we have spent so long trying to avoid, but which now, with in penitence and in faith, we must drink down.

Procession and Lament

The church travels through London. It does so daily as Christians crisscross the city, working and serving in every part of it. And the church does so formally and publicly, in its services and processions. As the church processes, it sings and it prays. As we see the city in turmoil around us, we pray a litany of repentance for the church's failure to pass on the good things of God.

The truth and dignity of mankind are held up by the church. Freedom is the gift that God gives to us, which makes us the image of God and which cannot be surrendered. Together the worshiping and lamenting church asks whether the body of this country, Britain, is being broken and scattered, or gathered, restored, and renewed. In its songs and prayers, it asks whether any community represented in these markets is being built up here or demolished.

On its journey through our city, the church must stop outside each business and pray for those who are serving there, and for those who are being served there, and for those whose products and labor are sold there. We lament when we see that any section of London, or of this nation of ours, is being ostracized and derided. We lament when we see that London is consuming or crucifying any other part, however distant, of the world, and however hard that violence is to identify. Whichever way the violence is going, we lament, for from these self-inflicted wounds our country is bleeding.

Every commercial service we offer one another is good, as long as it truly is a service. We ask whether it serves to divide each generation from its parents or to reconcile them. Christians can encourage all enterprise and commerce as particular forms in which we exercise our responsibility. But the church asks each enterprise and institution to examine itself and decide whether it gives the British hope and self-respect and all the qualities that make for a unified nation and an economy in which all can participate.

Nation on the Cross

We are led by the cross. Jesus is on the cross: he was crucified, for us. The cross shows us mankind in the throes of death. The cross reflects the violence around us and that we have inflicted on one another. The cross is a mirror, for the figure we see there is not just him but us. For it is our society that has put itself on the rack. It wants to love and to be loved, but it also fears, and it wants to remain in control, so be ready to withdraw from love. It does not want to receive the love of God, to whom all love belongs and to whom all love returns. It forms itself into a black hole of love rejected and turns into anger and misery. The figure on the cross is us, our society and our generation. We are the ones trapped in our rage and resentment and slowly engulfed by them. Each of us is a battleground on which our passions fight for possession of us. The body on the cross is the body of Britain. But the cross is not just inflicted on us; we are also the perpetrators of this misery. We inflict it on ourselves, and we inflict on each other. By denying this love, and bunching ourselves up into a refusal of love, we have constructed this rack and this prison cell, and by our denial that there is any wider, more spacious place beyond it we confine ourselves here.

But we, the British, are not on the cross on our own, without Christ. Even our utter determination to barricade ourselves against Christ cannot reduce or distance that love. Despite our attempts to run away from him, we are not left in our misery. Though we are on this cross, in this misery, and heading for this death and hell, he does not leave us here alone. He does not abandon us but remains here, standing with us. When we look into that cross, we may realize that he is here with us, and where the Lord is, there is his body also.

We are not left alone. The Lord is with us. And Christ takes on the full force and weight of the process of dissolution and lifts it from us. Alone, we are not able to withstand it. Christ is the only one who will finally suffer this crucifixion to the end. He will lift this appalling fate from every one of us. No one is left alone with this fate because Christ has taken it on in its entirety. Christ has suffered our crucifixion, so it has not actually touched us. The forces that we unleashed have not been allowed to make an end of us. He has taken our strife and death, lifted it, and taken it away from us.

As we watch our city, we see the crucifixion of mankind. But we also see this crucifixion lifted, removed, and replaced by the resurrection of Christ. Christ suffers here, and through his suffering, wrestles, overcomes, and subdues all the forces that we unleashed. In taking on the powers that we released, he is crucified and he continues to undergo this death until it is utterly extinguished. By this long crucifixion, we ourselves may survive what we unleashed and be raised.

The Gods of This World and the Degradation of Mankind

The church identifies all the activity we can observe in these streets as religious and cultic. We can lament the cruelty of delusion promoted by the love industries. We lament the disassociation and disengagement of generations. We lament the fathers who do not see children and the fatherless teenagers. We lament our disengagement from our parents' generation and the way we render them invisible in care homes and hospitals. We lament the partners not found, and we pray for those who have no wish to remain single. The church calls out for those men without women, women without men, and prays for the marriages that have not taken place. It laments the missing husbands and wives, the children unborn, and the population now sitting alone in front of a television.

Outside each business we may ask whether the body of Christ is being broken and so crucified again. We ask whether we have passed on the good things of God or withheld them. We may ask whether our failure has resulted in national self-harming—family breakup, abortion, fatherless young people turning tribal, disassociation from our own bodies, the sexualizing of our children and taking of childhood away so our children don't grow in imagination and character. The church laments all evidence of love rejected and substituted for.

These businesses are the cultic shrines of the gods of this world. They feed on mankind, and for them mankind is continually hauled onto the altar, carved open and splayed. He is divided: half is acceptable, half declared repellent and discarded. The gods demand it, and their spokesmen insist on it. Always a new fraction of him is revealed as morally too hideous to be permitted: his inadequacy and depravity is surely holding our society back. Man is divided again and again, from work, friends, and colleagues, from his body, from wife, from children, from parents, from his culture, from the last generation and the next, and from the traditions that give him his identity and self-worth. The regime continually invents new ways of dividing him, determining which of his aspects are threatening to them and turning public opinion against them. Everyone must show that they are appalled by this newly revealed vileness and agree that we urgently need to rid ourselves of him. Everyone watches their neighbor to check that they are on the right side. The everyday functioning of media, markets, and the economy are a pagan sacrifice. Their whole message is that for the sake of economic growth, for the sake of the gods of this world, mankind must be sacrificed and, at ever-decreasing intervals, sacrificed again.

This pagan sacrifice must be unmasked by the church. It must travel through societies fallen prey to cults, paralyzed by fear, convulsed by rage, vandalizing their culture and losing their mind. Our pilgrimage through these societies will be a way of the cross for us. As we bear it and suffer it, we will realize that many Christians in other generations have borne the cross through these streets before us. Their witness called those societies back to sanity and prevented the worst of their violence. Those saints gave their witness for us and were sometimes broken for us. At intervals on our procession, we arrive at a church or Christian foundation. We can celebrate in those places in which Christians in previous generations have reconciled their society and been instrumental in its healing. They are the wells along our route at which we can be glad about signs of the arrival of new reconciliation and wholeness in our society.

5. EUCHARIST—REDEEMED CREATION

The church is sent to the city to wait for Christ to appear. In its celebration of the eucharist, the church points to all the phenomena that signify the absence of Christ, and it looks for his coming again in glory. The church declares that Christ has died for us and has risen again to bring us his eternal life, and it points out that we see his passion continue here around us. It is the passion of mankind, yet the passion that Christ refuses to abandon us to, but which he takes on for himself, accompanies humanity through, and releases humanity from. The glory of mankind is established in Christ, but the glory of Christ is hidden in the passion and the ongoing life of the church and revealed in this cryptic way in the eucharist.

The world suffers and groans as it waits for its redemption. On the cross, Christ suffers the world, and the church is the form in which his body suffers, takes, and absorbs the violence of the world for us. In his person on the cross, the whole world travails as it waits for its redemption, in which the lost will be restored.

The Materiality of the Body

We receive the bread and wine as the gifts of Christ. For us they will become his body and blood. We live as material creatures who must take and consume other material creatures, plant and animal, in order to sustain ourselves. In the words of Ps 104:14, "He makes grass grow for the cattle, and plants for man to cultivate, bringing forth food from the earth: wine that gladdens the heart of man, oil to make his face shine and bread that sustains his heart." It is good for us to know where our own material sustenance comes from, and to acknowledge its goodness.

Every one of us is a material being, a creature of flesh, who requires inputs that he is unable to source for himself. Any city is dependent on the agriculture of this or some other country, and on the work of those who feed it, however little we know of them. Far away from this city, imagine a peasant farmer. He regards his animals as an investment and an achievement, as his savings and current account, and as the food that will feed his family. When these animals are eaten, their bodies will become part of his body and the bodies of his children. Their flock is their nourishment and sustenance; by next year some of these animal bodies will have turned into human bodies. As he looks at this flock or herd, he knows he is looking at the future of the bodies of his own people. What is so for him is true for us too.

In order that your body remains fit and healthy, something like the following events have to occur. A farmer takes his flock to market where they are bought by the wholesaler; the slaughterman turns them into carcasses; the butcher turns these into packets of meat. The wholesaler uses the services of insurers, vets, and food hygiene people, who attempt to reduce the risks in this process, and then a distributor and freight people. The transportation is supported by all those who pilot the ships and planes, and all those who service those craft and maintain that network, and all those who train them and police and protect them. The meat of this sheep traveled from that hillside to your plate because a hundred people operated the machinery by which this meat was packed in this box into this pallet, into this container and this trolley, and onto this display shelf.

The staples of our diet represent a great host of people. The sugar, chocolate, coffee, and everything else that stimulates our appetite and flavors our food are sourced from parts of the world with great economic and political challenges. We eat a thousand meals a year, each constituted by a dozen ingredients, sourced from every part of the world, each of which passes through the machine-minding hands of tens of people. Our bodies are therefore the product of thousands of workers, themselves supported by hundreds of thousands of others. At every point we can ask whether that employee earned enough to keep himself and his family, and to send his children to school. If he is not adequately paid, the question arises of whether we have been eating at his expense.

All this tells us that our body is not simply our own. It is a global product. When we consider that film-wrapped cut of meat in its little tray in the supermarket chiller-cabinet, we are looking at the work of this crowd. They may never meet, but their labor meets in this piece of lamb, and since we are now to eat this lamb, it meets in our body. The labor of all of these people has gone into us in this meal. We owe our own bodies to them, so their input gives them a stake in us. So now we have to ask whether we have eaten at their expense. Have they been built up by this process or exhausted and consumed by it? Have we eaten *with* them, or is it they who have been consumed in this process?

My body is made of what I have eaten. Eating does not merely sustain my body, but it creates it in the first place: my body is nothing but food, animated. I need my body in order to be locatable and available to you, and you to me. You have to find my body in order to find me. These animals make us present to one another, and the labor of these many hundreds of thousands of unseen people make us present to one another. You and I are only available to each other because we are physically and materially embodied, and this is because other people have served and contributed their labor to us. Our bodily presence to one another represent the years of other people's lives.

The Wrong Bread, the Wrong Cup

Human beings are creatures, and our bodies are made of other creatures. We are all dressed in flesh. But this flesh is not always ours in freedom, willingly given to us by those who have worked for it.

We may have consumed food unpaid for, made by workers never rewarded for it. We have to ask ourselves this question, before we hear that "The wages you failed to pay the workmen who mowed your fields are crying out against you. The cries of the harvesters have reached the Lord Almighty" (Jas 5:4). It may be that even the material of our own bodies belongs to others. Could it be that we are consuming them and when the Lord looks at us, he only hears their voices? We must ask ourselves this, so we never have to hear the words "Will evildoers never learn—those who devour my people as men eat bread and who do not call on the Lord?" (Pss 14:4; 53:4) This is particularly the question for the church here in the city of London, where the commodity markets are. Are the producers getting a fair price for their products? It is necessary to ask the question, however difficult it may be to answer.

We come to the altar with who knows what debts, our lifestyle sustained at what long-term cost. We do not know whether the food that has nourished and that ultimately constitutes our bodies has come from producers who have not been adequately recompensed and who are not adequately nourished. They need to be redeemed from us and to be restored, so that they too are dressed, gloriously, in all creation.

We need this debt to be cleared. Prayer to Christ cancels all unseen debts on the food and fuel that sustains us. Christ can release us from the workers who, under any form of coercion, have worked for us, and release them from us. But if we do not allow God to release these workers from us, we remain in debt to them. Ignorance or denial of these obligations means that we are in debt to powers we are not aware of. The body of Christ is still bound and being beaten. To this the church confesses that, by our disdainful or savage treatment of his little ones, we are defying Christ and still raging against him. Only when he mediates this world to us, releasing us from our debts to others, can even our own bodies become truly our own and sustain lasting relationships.

Two cups are set before us, the cup of the Lord and the cup offered by other masters. Since they have no resource of their own, other masters offer us what they have taken from others, so when we eat with them it may be at the expense of the poor. Our feast compels their fast. When we come to the altar, we do not know what debts we have. It may be that even the material of my own body belongs to others and that when my body appears at the altar it is their voices that God hears. We may not know, but we can surely ask, whether in this global economy we are sacrificing the poor in a pagan sense. "Should you not know justice, you who hate good and love evil; who tear the skin from my people and the flesh from their bones, who eat my people's flesh, strip off their skin and break their bones in pieces; who chop them up like meat for the pan, like flesh for the pot?" (Mic 3:1). Even if no one else does, it is the responsibility of the church to ask this question.

Christ Redeems the Poor from Us

The Lord regards the suffering of the poor as his own. He suffers because those that he regards as his own people and substance are wounded. He bears them and is covered in their blood. Because he has determined that they belong to him, their blood is his. Christ defends the poor from us who exploit them. He declares that he is "Against the shepherds and will hold them accountable for my flock. I will rescue my flock from their mouths, and it will no longer be food for them" (Ezek 34:7–10). Unless they ask for forgiveness, the exploiters will get back all the violence they doled out. "The Sovereign Lord says, 'Call out to all the wild animals: "Assemble and come together from all around to the sacrifice I am preparing for you. There you will eat flesh of mighty men and drink the blood of the princes of the earth as if they were fattened animals"'" (Ezek 39:17).

The Lord warns us that by exploiting and consuming the poor, we are aggressing, and continuing to crucify him. If the rich have not given the poor payment and release, the Sabbath they are owed, then the rich are consuming the poor and accruing for themselves a debt that they cannot pay. Their blood has become the blood of Christ. Only Christ can prevent this "cup of the wrath of the nations" from becoming the cup of judgment that we have to drink down. He alone can save us from the judgment of all those whose lives we have squandered and consumed. The church has to hear the Scripture: "Why are your robes all red, O Lord, and your garments like theirs who tread the winepress? 'I have trodden the winepress alone, and from the peoples no one was with me'" (Isa 63:2–3).

If we do not receive our sustenance from Christ, we become the function of other alien powers, famished, needy, resentful. If we do not eat only what Christ gives us, and ask him to pay those whom we have not paid or cannot pay, all our food may be a pagan sacrifice and an anti-eucharist that take away life from others.

The Eucharist as the Judgment of This World

God can extricate us from our vast and unresolvable debts to one another. He can release the rich from the poor, the consumer from the consumed, Dives from Lazarus. Our debts to one another are deep and unavoidable. We owe many people, unseen and unacknowledged, for our own existence.

If we do not acknowledge our debts, even our own bodies are forfeit. If we do not give our worship to God, we give ourselves away to other powers. Idolatry means giving yourself away to these gods and so supporting the claim that they are indeed forces we must obey, thereby deceiving and oppressing other people. They belong to God, and if we consume what is God's without receiving it from Christ, we are robbing them. We are filling the cup of judgment that will overflow and overtake us, so we will finally drink it all down ourselves. "The cup from the Lord's hand is coming round to you, and disgrace will cover your glory. The violence you have done will overwhelm you, for you have shed man's blood" (Hab 2:15). Only God can release us. The blood of Jesus is able to release from the multiple debts and bonds in which we all caught up.

This freedom from our rapacious consumption of one another is what the church celebrates in the thanksgiving of every eucharist. Only Christ's eucharist will redeem us from this consumption and destruction of one another that is the pagan eucharist always going on around us. The Christian people know that this release and forgiveness is there to be called upon, and they publicly and repeatedly call upon it.

6. WHOLE PEOPLE—MISERY AND DIGNITY

The body of Christ provides us with a lifelong series of encounters with the communion of the saints, and through them with the whole world.

The People of God Stand before the World

The Christian people stand and worship together before this society and so they are seen and heard by it. This is the commission given to the church. This witness of God to society is the purpose of the church. Evangelism and mission are manifestations of this fundamental purpose. Our witness comes both from going out to the world and from remaining where we are, standing and resisting the world that is determined to push us out. It is for their sake that we are here, setting out the truth and grace of Christ as the truth for mankind The church is the wall that protects society from despair, and we, who are the watchers on this wall, point our society to its coming Lord.

We are the troop that has been mustered here for our society, to be its guards and therefore soldiers. But Christ's army does not hurl or shoot anything. It simply marches and stands. It takes the incoming missiles thrown by a hurting world. Its armor is the truth, the faith, and the word of God (Eph 6:11–17). These are all the defence it has or needs. This army sings and offers the word of God. It tells the world that it does not need to throw these missiles, but it does so because it is in pain, and it is in pain because it is fighting the inevitability of its own repentance. The church may look as though it will soon break and disappear, but it never is broken. This is what the world finds so exasperating and offensive about it. The church simply stands here, and will do forever. This is why our Victorian hymn-writers make so much use of the words "yet" and "still," by which they mean "always" and unchangingly. With them we sing "dwell," "abide," and stay with us, Lord. We proclaim "his mighty resurrection and glorious ascension." The church is the salt that protects a society from decay and the leaven that keeps truth and hope percolating through that society.

Mankind Turned against Himself in Doubt and Despair

We are faced by the prospect of freedom and daunted by it. The Lord invites us to have freedom together with him. Freedom makes man the image of God, the counterpart of God. Freedom is not freedom *from* something or other, because what we are free *from* is always given to us or imposed on us. If it were so, every new circumstance would put us on the back foot, so we would always be backing off and afraid of what is coming next, and this fear would make us unfree. Freedom is freedom *for* someone. Freedom is accompanied by love, which means that it has a specific character, and that we are open and ready for whoever comes to us next.

We wonder whether we hear any voice but our own. Could God speak to us? Could we hear God? Along with all creation, we squirm in an agony of anticipation. Is God really calling us? Can God really turn creation into a willing partner, able to speak back and to decide freely with God and to receive God's work as good? God will judge us. We may not preempt that judgment. Fear makes us want to hide from any other judgment. This secular eschatology comes as the self-abasement of despair, or the self-exalting of limitless mastery, which can be terribly magnified through technology. We may doubt, reject, defy him, and despair.

But when our despair has run its course, God will still be here, and we can take what he offers us and so begin again.

We may want to believe that he is alone in the world. We are tempted to turn in on ourselves and give up. Our reservations towards the gospel, which come from fear, can turn to rage or into resignation, both of which can be given the most sophisticated and dignified expressions. Atheism is a form of panic or madness, badly covered up: it suggests that we have suffered a great disappointment. But we have not been disappointed, but are only afraid of being disappointed.

The result of taking on many of the images paraded before us by the secular liturgy is that each of us individually can feel overwhelmed and powerless. We may avoid this by surrendering regularly to Christ the burden of demands made on us by the entertainment industries and the torrent of images they deluge us with. Depression isolates us, making us believe that we are the only one who cannot cope. So, we pray for each who suffers depression, and we go to find each individual who has dropped out of sight.

Disdain for the Church

Christ considers the people of his kingdom to be his glory. The glory of a ruler is those who follow him in his parade. Christ has adopted as his troops those whom every other ruler has overlooked or scorned. Christ considers them his glory; we dare not consider them in any other way.

If we see only the inadequacy of the church, we are not yet looking at it as it will be. We must repent in order to receive the church as it truly is, as the body of Christ. The members of the church are the nonnegotiable form in which Christ comes to us. We have to receive them from him. They are Jesus, directly before us, but disguised. There is no way to him other than through them. In this very trying character, they are the hardness and difficulty of Jesus to us. We may not try to avoid them or control them. We may not distance ourselves from any part of the church, or decide that it is too old-fashioned, too quiet, too loud or in any other way unacceptable.

When we regard some church as exclusivist or fundamentalist, it may be we who are dividing, and rending, the body of Christ. This is just a desire to distance ourselves from those who have had fewer chances and less education than ourselves. It is to fail to realize that these people belong to Christ and have his protection and blessing. They are "the poor," who are most blessed. We have to regard these people as our preparation for Christ and master our exasperation with them in order to receive him.

To deride any part of the church is to turn away from Christ. Our identification of this or that part of the church as too liberal, or too evangelical, too traditionalist, too dogmatic, too narcissistic is simply to identity Christ as too unlike ourselves and so to reject this body by which he approaches us. We need to go to school with every other form of churchmanship and be taught by them. However poor in spirit and in understanding of the gospel any congregation is, however frankly mean-spirited, we have to recognize them as his. They are the weak brother for whom Christ died. To despise any part of the body is to reject its head.

In each of these unlovely people at the altar rail Christ says to us, "Do you see me yet? Do you love me?" The more repugnant they are, the more likely it is that Christ locates himself there, in them, for you. You have to embrace them as Christ, and you have to take their dislike and rejection of you. We have to learn the hard discipline of taking these people as the very gift and appearance of Christ. It is in this form that Christ has emptied himself, and in this form only that we may and must receive Christ. If they are the weak and we are the strong, it is we who have to be patient and wait for them (Rom 15:1). If we go ahead without waiting for anyone else, we fail to "recognize the body of the Lord" and so bring division into the church and judgment on ourselves (1 Cor 11:29, 33). Then the church becomes victim to a self-hatred that is directed against those least able to stand it. The degree to which we find one another unattractive and un-Christlike is the result of the dark and incomprehensible way, crucifying our expectations, in which Christ gives us his presence.

Christ Unrecognized in the Darkness of the Cross

Christ is exalted. To us, however, this exaltation looks like a descent and abasement. He is seated in glory, seen in the epiphanies seen by Moses, Isaiah, and Daniel, the divine figure whose holiness appears like fire. But to us this radiant holy one appears as this figure on the cross, and so as this horror, from whom we want to look away. The Lord whom they saw, high and lifted up, appears to us only as this image of destruction. Mankind is reduced to nothing before our eyes by some unspeakable force. To the unholy, he is this picture of horror. The church that points to this sight appears to belong to an ancient and incomprehensible past, redolent of dark powers, and therefore as something that we should have nothing to do with. For all the world it looks as though the church has been abandoned and left sitting in ashes, destitute. This is the judgment of the world. Could it be right? Could this also be the judgment of God? Will God confirm the judgment of the pagans on the church? If the Lord has turned away, the light is going, and the world will become a more hostile place to everyone in it.

We have to plead with the Lord to avert or reverse this judgment. We have to beg him to stay here with us and not let us have the consequences of our action. He could give up on us, take his blessing away from us. Would he abandon us so that our nation receives no witnesses, so that there is no church in this country, until finally there would be no country either?

The church is given to the world in order to serve it. It may do this by telling each people and nation who they are, telling them that Christ recognizes and knows them and is the true guardian of their identity. When it does not pass on Christ, the truth of its life, the church betrays the world, leaving it exposed to the predators, so that each nation is left to become a broken and bleeding body.

Our nation is only a single political community because the gospel has brought this unity to it. When no gospel is heard here, this nation will break up into communities identifiable by age groups and ethnicities, each regarding others as a burden it does not need and organizing itself against them. When the witness of the church disappears, society divides until it is no longer a single community, but only rival tribes again.

What we see in church teaches us what to see outside church, in our offices and business and the streets of our cities. Mankind is with God, for God is with mankind. But each person we see strangely sees him or herself only as someone-on-their-own, with whom God has no relationship. Everywhere we find people who imagine themselves deserted by God, and who believe that they deserve to be deserted. They do not allow themselves companions for fear that they would be opening themselves to God, from whom all companionship comes.

We have to tell them that God is with them and that the glory of God shines on them, and into them, and even shines back out of them again to us. This is the view we see. But to say so and to see it so takes practice, and so in church we recalibrate our eyesight and practice this vision.

Above the Cross, the Glory

In church we see two views, one above the other. Let us imagine that as we come into church, we find ourselves standing before a screen that hangs from the ceiling and stretches across the building from one side to the other. We can walk under it, so as we come further up the aisle towards the altar, we see that there is another screen above it. From the back of the church, by the entrance, we can only see the lower screen, and until we come further in, we would never know that there is this second screen above it. This lower screen shows us the cross, and all the action of the passion and death of Jesus. There is Jesus crucified, in that place of utter and final abandonment that we are all afraid of. There, lamenting, are his mother Mary and John and Mary Magdalene, each frozen in their own misery. Christ's killers look on, each also a rictus of pain, and there further back are the people of Jerusalem, their faces displaying grief and shock; behind them are the gentiles, their faces showing rage and fear. All these figures reveal the truth of us in this moment and of our present political regime. Christ crucified is an image of the compressed violence and pain of the world, the pain we inflict on one another and that rebounds on ourselves. Christ on the cross is Christ "according to the flesh," that is, as the world judges. This corresponds to the way that the world sees Christ as this ambiguous lonely figure far back in the past.

But as you walk on under this image of crucifixion, you see a vaster image above it. High above us is the image of Christ who has overcome death and is risen and victorious. This second image, which shows Christ in glory, also portrays us there with him and around him. Is this a view of our future? It is certainly the image that puts the question of our future. Are we with him? What is the relationship of the two images on the two screens? Christ in glory comes to us in the form of this figure of Jesus incarnate, and suffering and finally crucified.

God Glorifies Mankind

Now imagine that as you come into church these two images superimpose themselves, like a hologram. You see Christ, high and lifted up, but each time you take a step nearer, you find only that the exalted Lord moves further away. Now the view seems to take you downwards, as though the floor of the church started sloping rapidly away before you, so any move you make towards the altar turns into a slide down this slope towards ignominy, isolation, and distress. This is how our progress towards resurrection is: it is a descent into this passion. Our salvation comes as a great humbling. The lower screen, in which Christ hangs on the cross, shows us how we may receive Christ glorified. As we look at this scene of horror it becomes clear that this is not Christ's horror or violence but our own, and yet now it is no longer our own either, because Christ has taken it from us. As we continue to look at this figure on the cross, it is obvious that he is not isolated or abandoned, but rather that the cross exalts him and is his throne. He is entirely and confidently with the Father, and the Spirit surrounds him with the whole company of heaven and so vindicates him. With Christ all this good company has poured itself into the narrow compass of mankind and into the unimaginably alien form of mankind uprooted, cut off from his history and origins, isolated from all creation and made unrecognizable by death. Though he goes through this alien form for our sake, Christ and all his company are indissolubly united in the communion of God. We are no longer isolated, or defaced and disfigured, but reunited, redeemed, and glorified. We will come back to this theme in our last chapter.

In Christ, God is glorifying mankind. This is what the vision in the book of Revelation is showing us. "Behold, a great multitude which no one could number, from every nation, from all tribes and peoples and tongues, standing before the throne and the Lamb. They were clothed in white robes and had palms in their hands, and they cried with a loud voice, saying, 'Salvation belongs to our God who sits on the throne, and to the Lamb'" (Rev 7:9–10). So, we may pray: "May God in his infinite love and mercy bring the whole church, living and departed in the Lord Jesus, to a joyful resurrection and the fulfilment of his eternal kingdom."

Chapter 4 in Summary

1. **Since the church is the witness of God to the society to which it is sent, it worships out in the public square, where the world can watch and hear.**

2. **Christians withdraw from the world to pray, and the world is intrigued.** The world watches, wants the qualities that they have, and follows them.

3. **Those who are formed by Christian worship develop self-control and cease to be needy advocates of their own interests.** Their well-ordered lives are recognized and emulated, and the rule of law and liberal political culture emerges. Private virtues create public virtues. The mediation of the church maintains the fragile unity of the nation.

4. **The church is the source of public service.** Those who govern themselves well are able to help other people to do the same. From individual self-government emerge the rule of law, public service, and national identity. All government originates in the self-government of individuals that gives rise to individual public service.

5. **Christian worship gives rise to the secular public sphere and the practices of public speech.** These include good counsel, individual conscience, record-keeping, and the public administration of justice. These create trust and confidence and respect for the individual, his work and property. This confidence makes it possible to take risks, to explore and discover, and develop the culture that pursues knowledge and science, and from which industry and prosperity come.

6. **Love aspires to permanence and so seeks the correction and discipleship that will make it permanent.** When we exercise self-restraint, then we can act generously and for other people. The church teaches self-control and the ability to wait. Christian discipleship sustains our self-giving permanently.

7. **Christian discipleship and discipline must be learned and taught.** Those who commit themselves to this vocation are our clergy, educators, and academics. Those who listen to the whole people of God will remain faithful servants, while others risk becoming stumbling

blocks. Teachers of the church who do not pass on the whole deposit of faith, and fail to hear those who are suffering, risk the salvation of a whole generation.

8. **The church celebrates the passion and resurrection by travelling publicly on its way of the cross.** It travels to Easter through the passion of Lent, in which it withdraws in order to prepare for the trials that this witness requires. When it processes through our city and society, the church has to address that society with prayers, asking all sections of our society whether they are able to sustain or only undermine the dignity that God has given to mankind.

9. **The church repents for its failure to be the holy witness that the world waits to see.** The community that is made strong by the resurrection can suffer, allow itself to remain vulnerable, repent, and ask for forgiveness. It can lead the repentance of the nation and say what that nation cannot say for itself. The church is the community in which forgiveness is seen at work, in which trust is generated and the social capital of a nation restored.

10. **When the church fails to proclaim the resurrection, the world suffers a passion that is without hope of redemption and so is unending.** Mankind is continually redivided into antagonistic communities, in which the powerless are scapegoated and expended by the powerful.

11. **The church has to name the powers and diagnose our crises.** It does so by relating them to the high concept of mankind that comes from the gospel, or to the reduced concepts of mankind used by those cults and sensibilities that present themselves as secular (defined by opposition to the gospel), which, disengaged from truth and goodness (and beauty), reduce every question to the single issue of power.

12. **The liturgy of the world declares that we must extricate ourselves from society and make ourselves alone. Each of us must raises ourselves above all others.** We have no fellows and are only ever threatened by other people. Either utter isolation is your destiny or loss of self-awareness and individuality through absorption within the mob.

13. **The liturgy of God celebrates that man is established in his dignity and distinctiveness, in his individuality and in good company.** We

acknowledge where our identity comes from, so we are content and give thanks. Our thanksgiving is what our service of worship is, and this worship is our service to our neighbors and the wider world.

14. **Giving credit where it is due is the Christian public service.** Christians give thanks to God to whom it is owed and withhold their praise from all other authorities that claim too much for themselves.

15. **We withhold credit whenever it has been falsely attributed.** We do not give tribute to any authorities that demand it, no matter how threatening they become, when they do not concede that we must primarily give thanks and praise to God.

16. **Our prayers are a form of public prophecy that addresses the powers and institutions of our nation, warning them not to take for themselves divine powers.** The Christian doctrine of God is our defence against false gods and demonic powers.

17. **We may confess and repent on behalf of the powers that be.** We can invite them to give glory to God and so stop damaging our nation by their defiance of God. By our worship we keep the pressure on the powers that be and so keep them under control.

18. **The church names the forces of disintegration at work in the nation.** The church tells the society in which it lives that it has no need to torment and divide itself but may receive its restoration from the covenant made public in the resurrection of Christ.

19. **The world is presently being torn apart and dismembered in a pagan sacrifice.** And it is the world that is doing this tearing. It is self-inflicted, but it is also always inflicted most painfully by those with the power to do so, and most particularly against those without any worldly power to resist.

20. **The church asks the society to which it is sent whether it is consuming those who serve it.** It asks this society whether it is itself undergoing the same division and destruction. The church points out that, in the long term, those who only consume may be consumed.

21. **The penitent church asks whether the nation is being broken and scattered, or gathered, restored, and renewed.** In its songs and prayers, it asks whether any community represented in these markets is being built up here or demolished.

22. **The world is not secular but cultic.** Our secularizing elite claims that Christianity is religious and therefore irrational; only what has been deracinated and so purified of all connection to the past can be rational, it believes. Christians reply that this very claim, that there is a duty of continuous secularization, is religious; as much as any regime cuts itself from every tradition of thought, it is unable to reason or to acknowledge any cultural givens at all, and so may end in a mankind-destroying frenzy.

23. **The church is the necessary voice within any society.** The church includes those who are not acknowledged or represented by in any other institution, so it is the articulate and the inarticulate and disenfranchised together. People from all stations of society stand shoulder to shoulder and kneel and confess their sins together. It is the embodiment of the reconciliation of all opposites and so is the present anticipation of the future reconciliation of all mankind.

5

The Church for the Long Term

1. GATHERING—THE UNITY OF THE CHURCH

On Sunday the whole Christian people are gathered together in one place. Each church is given to one particular society by God, and must stand in that society, and be visible and audible to it. Their unity comes to them from beyond them and is embodied by the figure who stands at their head.

The Church Is Apostolic

When the church gathers, it does so around one Christian, for whom we will use the two traditional terms of "apostle" and "bishop." Literally, the apostle is the person who is sent; the church has sent this Christian to us. When we gather around him, the church is an image of all the apostles gathered around Christ. Or we could refer to the function of oversight (episcopé) or supervision that this Christian has, from which the word "bishop" (episcopos) comes. He watches to ensure that we remain faithful to the whole teaching of the church and so remain orthodox and catholic.

One Christian can play this role for all of us, because in the Christian faith the single figure is fundamental. Humans do not start to become important only when there are lots of them, but each of us is fundamentally significant in his absolute uniqueness. We could take any member of the congregation and set them before us. The worldwide church could send us anyone they choose for us, but, having received him, he is then the one we gather around.

Since the bishop stands at the center of our gathering, he is the view we see, the visible embodiment of the presence of Christ for us. But why should it be the bishop who is the central figure for the whole church? Many churches use other terms for him—minister, priest, vicar—and regard these as sorts of "clergy." Often discussions of ministry start with the priest, and after comparing lower and higher conceptions of priesthood, consider the bishop as a priest with additional responsibilities. Instead, we will look at the bishop first and then at other minsters as representatives of him.

Can this concentration on this single Christian be right? Many communities of Christians do not want to acknowledge a single Christian leader. Some communities emphasize that the gifts of leadership are spread across a team of leaders. Some may object that a particular bishop does not seem to have the Spirit's anointing or lacks the Spirit's more conspicuous gifts. If he appears a remote figure, how can he appeal to the whole community and above all to the young church?

Many Christian communities are founded by one charismatic leader. He may attract great numbers and build a community in which many of the gifts of Christ are evident. But what understanding of charismatic is then at work? Do we regard him as a leader even when neither he nor we know how to distinguish between spiritual discipleship and other more conspicuous gifts that attract numbers of followers but which indicate a more worldly success? If he does not give any public acknowledgment of the discipline of the whole catholic church, what authority is this leader himself under? How can his people be confident in his leadership if it does not know the standards against which he should be tested, and if that leader himself does not acknowledge those standards? Does he concede that he is accountable to those outside his own community who are competent to judge him and call him to account?

For such charismatic communities there is a succession problem. When the identity of the community depends on its love of its leader, what happens when he dies? How does it find another charismatic figure to replace him? Many such Christian communities do not survive beyond the second generation of leaders. But where there are traditions and structures, the issue of succession does not bring a crisis. The test of whether the leader is truly charismatic, that is, whether he displays all the gifts of the Spirit given to the Church, is whether he himself is a good disciple, and indeed, whether he stands out by his discipleship, and this means by his deference to the Church that is beyond his community. He must submit to the whole body of Christ, the Church that he cannot control.

We may not like the leader who stands before us. We may only be able see his faithlessness. But we have to take him and tell him that we accept him, as the gift of Christ to us, the apostle for this time and place. The figure Christ places in front of us is seldom the one we find easy or impressive or the one we would have chosen. Leadership in the Church is a difficult issue because Christ sends us those apostles who are least flattering or plausible to us, and therefore most humbling.

The bishop makes visible the truth that every Christian stands before every other Christian, begging for reconciliation with them. As the bishop stands before the world, offering it Christ, so he reminds us that every Christian is Christ himself standing before the world and offering himself to it. The bishop is a public demonstration of our vocation and the vulnerability that comes with it.

Reconciliation and Catholicity

Every one of us is a member of the whole church of Christ. The Christian life and faith are the sole path to our universal reconciliation. The gospel brings the reconciliation of every household and community with every other, so we can say that catholicity, or ecumenism, is simply what the gospel achieves. We are catholic as we look towards our reconciliation with all other Christians and churches. We must pray for them, mention them in our intercessions, and mourn our separation from them. But we must also treat them as those who have some portion of Christ, and so as those we must learn from and submit to. In the apprenticeship of this Christian life, we learn to reach out to the whole of the rest of the church, indeed to the future completion of the church, when Christ shall be all in all.

The bishop is not therefore only an office-holder of the Catholic or Anglican or "episcopalian" church, that is, of the churches that use this job title. He is bishop to every church and ecclesial community. The office of bishop is ecumenical because it is the office of Christ who calls all men to unity, and since it is Christ who calls, we must hear and obey. Ecumenism is not an option that may or may not be taken, but the command of the Lord; it is his assertion, for our sake, of his lordship. Superintendents and moderators of Methodist or Presbyterian churches can concede that functionally they are bishops by another name.

We are under many authorities in the church, but the bishop is all these authorities conveniently brought together in one person. You can go and speak to him and tell him whatever is on your mind. He is an apostle, one of the Twelve, here for us. He is our spiritual giant, our "reverend Father in God." We have to demand some blessing and wisdom, some correction and warning from him each time we see him. We must ask him to lead us and remind him that he is surrounded by a great cloud of witnesses. As the Ordination service tells us, bishops "are to govern Christ's people in truth, lead them out to proclaim the good news of the kingdom and prepare them to stand before him when at last he comes in glory."

The bishop stands in the church, surrounded by his people, and speaks from it, and primarily he speaks to it. He does not speak primarily to the world, and he certainly does not speak to the world without the church, or intimate that he has anything to offer other than what the church offers to the world. The bishop speaks to the church, and the church speaks to the world. Any minister of the church that bypasses the church in their public pronouncements mistakes the source of their authority. In his own diocese, and particularly standing within his own cathedral, the bishop is the presence of the whole church and therefore the presence of Christ for us. His authority and responsibility have been given him by Christ, so he is therefore responsible to Christ for us. He must exercise his authority with all gentleness, lamenting his unworthiness, but he must exercise that authority. When he does not lead, the church suffers. We have to beg him to love us and give us all that Christ has entrusted to him for our sake. "With the shepherd's love they are to be merciful but with firmness, to minister discipline but with compassion," in the words of the Church of England ordination service.

The Apostle Leads the Worship

The bishop leads the worship of the church. He prays and intercedes for his people, and he leads the intercessions of the people, in public, in the eucharist. He stands between them and their sins, and he names their sins and repents of them on their behalf.

The first job of the bishop is to pray. He has to show us how to value the prayers and forms of worship that have been handed down to us, and he can compose prayers, litanies, intercessions, and hymns that are in continuity with them. He has to teach his people to pray and worship and lead their intercessions for the world.

The bishop teaches his people the doctrine of the whole church. He must come to each congregation with questions and correction, and give them the word that fits the season and addresses our situation. He does not simply give each congregation a pat on the head, or adopt their particular brand of churchmanship for the day, but brings them what they do not yet have. He is to train and discipline us; this discipline is fundamental to our being made holy. He must examine us, as any military leader tests the readiness of his troops and the strength of his defenses. When Christians push at the church to see how much transgression they can get accepted, the bishop must call them to account and identify their behavior as sin, or he leaves his people weakened.

We are not left alone, but in Christ we are now to be shaped, molded and loved, by the whole church, and so by whole historical tradition and worldwide catholicity that belongs to the body of Christ. This church has authority over us for our sake, to make disciples of us. Whenever a church refuses any part of these gifts and disciplines and sets out to found its faith on something less than the full deposit of faith, the bishop will exercise the discipline that will bring it back to obedience, and he will endure the suffering that this will involve. Their love of him will grow because of this discipline. In order to give discipline, the bishop himself must have received it and live under it. He must continually refer to the whole tradition of the church that we are all under and show how much lighter it is than the insidious worldly burdens to which we are otherwise drawn.

Gathering around Our Apostle

The bishop is the public face of the church. We must ask him to speak, pray, and bless us and our city from the steps of his cathedral on festivals. We need to accompany him out onto the steps so that surrounded by all our priests and ministers, he can speak from the church to the world.

We must gather around him so it is clear that he speaks for us, and when he speaks, he says what we all say, which is what the whole church has always said. The bishop must quote publicly from the worship and documents of the church; he must issue bishop's letters at the beginning of each season of the church year that can be read from pulpits and studied by house groups. He must relate all his public statements in the worship of all the people who make up the church and end every public meeting and interview by praying for his city and pronouncing the blessing of God on it. He is the corporate and embodied ecclesial life, visible as one person; for this reason, his deacons and people must stand at his side.

The bishop can function as our pastor only as we continually encourage him to do so. He is subject to the same pressures and uncertainties as any other Christian, so we need to give him confidence so that he can serve us and speak in our name without reserve. He must tell us what we need to hear, and we must demand to hear it from him. We pray for him and for our ministers every time we meet, and we tell them so, and remind them whenever we speak to them, of the power of God to make them holy. The respect and love that his people have for their bishop should be evident.

The Apostle Unrecognized

When any church celebrates the eucharist it must acknowledge that it is doing so as part of the whole church and therefore with every Christian congregation. As demonstration of that unity, we could for example send some eucharistic bread, blessed rather than consecrated, round to every other church in the city, and ask them to send us their blessing and encouragement from us. The bishop must go to every church of every denomination, to those who do not recognize his authority, as well as those who do, and knock on the door of every Christian community in his diocese, not only of those churches that recognize bishops, but of those that claim their freedom from hierarchy, and so to every independent assembly and house church.

The bishop must stand outside each church and knock, offering himself to those who have not asked for him, and say "I came to those who did who did not call for me . . . all day long have I held out my hands to an obstinate people" (Isa 65:1–2). He must wait outside each Christian community until they relent and let him in. As long as he waits, he is an image of the whole church, suffering and waiting, and a public sign that Christ is presently waiting for each assembly to let his body in. The bishop has to lead the repentance for the divisions in the witness of Christ in the various reductions of the gospel into ethical agendas or aesthetic sensibilities that tempt congregations away from the orthodoxy and catholicity of the church. He has to beg forgiveness for their separation and aloofness, and with them he has to look forward to celebrating together at last. Every eucharist looks forward to this and every exchange of the peace anticipates it.

At our worship, at the altar, elders or deacons gather around the bishop, as the disciples gather around the Lord. This relationship of Lord and people, the head and the body, is the fundamental image that makes our witness visible. These several witnesses point to this single figure, who is their head. The whole body, and thus all Christian people together are a single unit of priesthood when gathered around their head. Their agreement demonstrates that the church is the truly catholic body and that all other communities are partial, not yet the whole truth. Our way into this truly universal communion is through the cross of Christ which removed all false universals from us. We may now know Christ only together with every single one of those whom he brings with him.

2. HEARING—SERVANTS OF THE WORD

The whole Christian community hears the word of God. The word comes with the order and authority that enables the church to receive it. The church ordains particular people to authority so that they can pass on to us the words that the church has received from all previous Christian generations and prevent us from going in directions that take us away from the historic and worldwide church.

The worship of the church is the source of Christian teaching. All theology is commentary on what the church hears and sings. We read Scripture in the company of all the Christians who have preceded us. We have to chew on it, and through meditation and contemplation let it do its work. All the sanctified teachers of the church who have read these Scriptures before us are available to help us in this. We may discover from them how Christians have been shaped by these Scriptures to endure through brutal times, and remained faithful to the point of martyrdom. If we listen to all the witnesses of the many generations, from the fathers of the early church to the Christians who withstood the totalitarianisms of the twentieth century, we will persevere in this long apprenticeship. Otherwise, we will only be reading Scripture through the untaught eyes of our contemporaries, and be as exposed as they are to the forces blasting through our present generation.

Ministers of Word and Sacrament

It is the job of every minister to witness to this service of Christ to us. Christ serves everyone, but he serves his body especially in that he reveals this service to us and allows us to participate in it. The distinction between the church and the world is a foretaste of the resurrection. We serve our society by explaining the differences between the church and the world, not by minimizing the distinction between them.

The laity are secular, for they are out "in the world." To use an old distinction, we "laypeople" are "secular," out in the world, while our clergy are "religious," withdrawn from the world and committed to the work of God's worship. Our ministers and clergy serve us by freeing us for service of the world. They do so by leading us in this service, teaching us the discipleship that makes it possible, and by showing us how to participate in this service of Christ's. They must remind us constantly of our new identity as servants of the world and help us to take and lay down before the Lord all the sin of the world. We come into church, through the cleansing water that flows from the font; our ministers help us to confess and be rid of all the accumulated detritus of the week, or possibly of years. Like a wrestler's seconds, when we gather on Sunday morning, our ministers mop our brows and tell us that we are doing well and that Christ is fighting for us. They tell us that we are being made holy through this grueling service and we can let go of the sin that sticks to us.

We have been forgiven. Just as our life is no longer ours to live alone, so our problems and sin are not ours any longer. We are free to seek more and more of that forgiveness, to do so with increasing confidence and more and more publicly. We are free to confess our sins publicly and to lead those around us in letting go of their sins. We are free for others, and so we may be the most carefree people. We may serve at tables, fetch and carry, wait at hospital beds, find words of comfort for the anguished and frightened, anoint the dying.

Our Lord is free. He is so entirely free that he can do the things that we most associate with loss of freedom. He does not regard his divinity as something that he has to hold on to, but taking the inconspicuous form of a servant, he has made himself nothing (Phil 2:5). This servanthood is for those into whose hands Christ has given all things. This weight of glory is ours. It releases us from having to busy ourselves first with our own affairs before turning, with whatever strength we have left, to help others. We do not need to look for glory or confirmation, for we have it, and we need never concern ourselves about it again.

As the people come into church their ministers can say to them, "Put your load down here and rest. Eat and drink here what will give you back your strength." Ministers will baptize and teach, hear confession, marry people, and bury them. The laity are out and about in the world all week long. They come to church to recover the holiness that is promised to them, not only for their sake but also for the sake of all those whose griefs they bear. As they leave the service, the minister may stand by the door and tell the congregation as they go back out that they are holy, and that this holiness empowers them to bear the sin of others and bring it to the Lord to be removed forever.

The church is given ministers who are educated and ordained to open the Scripture and administer the sacraments to us. In the words of the Church of England ordination service, they are to "unfold the Scriptures, to preach the word in season and out of season, and to declare the mighty acts of God." They have promised that they be "diligent in prayer, in reading Holy Scripture, and in all studies that will deepen their faith and fit them to bear witness to the truth of the Gospel." If they do so we will grow in confidence in the intellectual robustness of the teaching on the eucharist and the work of Christ in atonement and in all the doctrine of the church that has been passed down to us. These words, and the quotations in the remainder of this section, come from the Church of England ordination service, which is at least as complete as, and has no substantial differences from, the ordination services of other churches.

Our ministers are ordained to "lead God's people in the offering of praise and the proclamation of the Gospel." They are to "sustain the community of the faithful by the ministry of word and sacrament that we all may grow into the fullness of Christ and be a living sacrifice acceptable to God." They are to explain to us what we ourselves have been singing, so that we can sing it with increasing understanding and gladness. They will "lead Christ's people in proclaiming his glorious Gospel, so that the good news of salvation may be heard in every place." They have vowed to do this "by the help of God." God has undertaken this for us, and these ministers are the form in which he has promised to do so.

The clergy are to teach us how to pray and to worship, so that they can say "What I received from the Lord I also handed on to you" (1 Cor 11:23). This worship is the act of the whole Christian people, so the teaching of this worship and the formation of those who are to lead us in it must be accountable to the whole church.

The minister will point out to each congregation that they are being made holy and distinct from the world. They will use all the hymnody and prayers of the church, and the iconography of the church buildings, to teach them the holy and priestly identity of the church. They will teach us our prayers so that we can say them off by heart. Priests will introduce their congregation to the saints of church who preceded us, and so they will teach us our place in the Christian body and its public pilgrimage through the world. They will visit the house of every parishioner, pray and bless it, and bring an image of the saint of that church to be displayed in that home. The church must honor its own recent teachers, by naming them in our intercessions, teaching us their story and displaying pictures of them in church.

When speaking to those outside the church, the clergy must affirm that they say only what the whole church says, and refer to the worship, liturgy, and documents of the whole catholic church. The ordained Christian life is one of study that prepares us for witness and that enables to identify and confront those oppressive constructions and forms of behavior in society at large. We study in order to be able to name the powers that are arrayed against us, so that we can protect those who cannot protect themselves. These are the privileges of those Christians ordained to the public service of the church.

The Deposit of Faith

The teaching of the church is the teaching of Christ. In knowledge of him we find true knowledge of ourselves. He himself is our teacher; his teaching is the "Word of truth" and the "breastplate of righteousness" (Eph 6). It brings light to the darkness in which we have been living. Tradition is the "deposit of faith" that has been handed on to us. If we do not pass it on, it is then the coin that we bury in the ground (Matt 25:25) because we assume that God is an uncaring master, unmoved by whether we live or die. If we bury this truth, we bury the hopes of those who might expect to receive this faith from us and with it their own identity and salvation.

The clergy must honor the whole church and present their gospel for the affirmation of the whole church. They must do so in the face of that other rival "theology" that sees the church as old and the Spirit as new, and assumes that we always have to give up whatever it identifies as established or old. Such a theology follows the spirit of the age and contrasts charisma to institution and promotes activism over worship, aesthetics over mission, or individual spirituality over the given and "established" institutional forms of our ecclesial life. It will regard all previous generations of Christians as ignorant.

But the past and the future may not be pulled apart in this way, for the Spirit who raised Christ from the dead also holds all communities, of the past and of the future, together. Christian clergy must be able to distinguish themselves from the "secular" account that sees freedom in terms of freedom from our past. We have a long Christian history that we can learn from. The church that attempts to reinvent itself by slicing away parts of its own tradition in the hope of finding some new and more acceptable point of contact with society will betray that society utterly.

The church encourages our society to examine what previous generations have given us and so to realize that they also faced the issues we face. Thus, we understand that those issues that our contemporaries regard as new are not new. We can then shed the self-impoverishing assumption that our generation has reached the summit of human knowledge and can give up the knowledge acquired by previous generations of Christians.

The experience that we associate with the contemporary church is not new. God is consistent. Though they are past, present, or future to us, all his acts work to unite us with previous and future generations as one people, and so make us a people no longer divided by time. To this end we need to learn the virtue of patience, of suffering and intellectual discipleship. We need to go to previous generations to be taught by them. Through centuries of debate, the church has developed a theology of the gathered community and of the individual Christian. All God's people are given to us to love, so we must love them, and surrender all desire to place ourselves above the church, that is, above the people whom God has called together as Christ's body.

Imitation Gospels

The gospel gives us freedom. It is always offered in the face of rival gospels. When freedom, justice, or any other virtue is exalted over the gospel it becomes part of some ideology and ceases to be gospel.

Equality is no substitute for the gospel. The *dignity* of every human being is not the same thing as the *equality* of every human being with every other. The church teaches that our value is secured by proper order and authority and therefore also by real differences between us. We select and ordain ministers, who then have authority over us, so we must acknowledge that there must indeed be this hierarchy of authority and excellence. We must insist that they live up to their calling, which means that we must have the courage to challenge them (2 Cor 10:1–2). There are gifts and virtues that neither we nor our ministers yet have, but which we must seek for each other's sake. It is only the elevation of one Christian as this ordained minister that allows the rest of us to be a single body, made so by the mutual subordination in love by which we are able to become servants of one another and, in this sense, "equal" to one another.

The gospel presents us with a very large account of humanity. It tells us that we are called by God, who waits for us to turn to him in response, and that every person we encounter is a gift that God has given to us. The gospel teaches us both that we hold out against our fellow human beings, even though they are given to us in order to form our future, and that we therefore need the salvation that will bring us into communion with them.

Church and University

The church refers to mankind as a wonder and a mystery. It insists on asking about his dignity and his calling. "What is man, that you should be mindful of him; the son of man, that you should seek him out?" (Ps 8:4). The worship of the church taught generations of our ancestors to wonder about and explore all relationships of God, mankind, and creation that this worship taught him. In the course of voicing creation's praise, the worshipping community reflects on the creation that was said to praise God. After their worship, and as a result of it, the worshipers and wonderers came together in a body to explore and debate this creation. This wonder brought into being a great project of inquiry that we now call the university. Over generations the worshipers and wonderers who gathered together in this way as the university began to specialize in particular forms and departments of knowledge. The clergy became academics, and their particular concerns became the various disciplines and sciences of the university. The church was shaped by the wonder that is the origin of all curiosity and science, and the sparks that flew from the church created the university.

For a long time, the church held its vast view of mankind together. But, little by little, it let this unified view lapse into separate accounts and separate sciences. It ceased to set out its vast view of mankind as this united creature that we should wonder at. And as it ceased to hear the church, the university was no longer informed by wonder and ceased to regard man both as a being within creation, and then as a creature with a unique dignity. It no longer asked the question, put by Ps 8:4, "What is man, that you should be mindful of him?"

With little or no relationship to worship and wonder, distinct areas of knowledge within the university became fenced off from one another. The worship that defines the relationship of God and mankind became separated from the relationships of man with mankind described by the disciplines of ethics and politics. It separated the relationship of man and the world created by economics and technology, from knowledge of our natural environment, now termed simply science. Christian worship held these concerns together. But when all reference to that wonder and worship was given up, these became separate fields, which not only divided up knowledge of the world but also our understanding of humanity.

Slowly the church allowed its doctrine to be stripped from it. Christ was no longer worshiped as the true man and truth of mankind and guarantor of the dignity of man: in Christ, God had once visited us, but then returned to a deistic distance from us. The church then delegated the doctrine of creation to the university so that this ceased to be a doctrine and became knowledge without reference to wonder, and so no regard for its own limits or purpose. The church acquiesced in much-reduced definition of religion as the discourse of the inner world of the individual and gave up talking about man in creation. It allowed the university to reduce its account of Christ until he was a merely religious phenomenon, situated within a history of religion, of no great public or rational significance.

Once the sparks that came from wonder at mankind and creation flew from the church to create the university. Now the occasional spark flies back from the university to the church, each insight part of a now-fractured vision of man as creature of God. But since they are not reconnected to the church's understanding of us as respondent and worshiper of God, these are not recognized as the church's own insights returning to it. Each briefly starts a fire in the church and then burns out to leave a hole in the fabric of our teaching.

The unity of man comes from outside him, from God. But when this is not acknowledged, there are attempts to secure the identity of man through scientific and technological effort. When control through technologization replaces wonder, the integrity and identity of man is lost, and what is human is broken up into distinct issues and problems for which separate social sciences identify technological solutions that increasingly treat man without dignity. When man is no longer regarded as chief wonder of God, wonder becomes an embarrassment, and the freedom of man becomes a problem.

The contemporary university opposes itself to the church that expresses this wonder in public academic form. Christian theology reminds the humanities what they are about. Without it, the humanities no longer know what their agenda is, so they pursue the chimera of equality into increasingly illiberal attitudes, and sensing their own intellectual vulnerability, come to resent Christian theology. The institution now dedicated to human formation is reluctant to tolerate any particular definition of that formation. When educationalists tell us that there is no master narrative and no right answer, they remove from the debate the means by which we can discuss their claims. By insisting that the debate is completely open and anyone can believe everything and cannot be corrected, they close debate down. If the church lets it, the university usurps the place of the church and becomes a false "church" and a new totalitarianism.

The Church Defends the Dignity of Man

Mankind is the wonder of God, appointed by God to be the chief wonderer at all God does. We must be roused to watch and wonder at all that is around us. When we do not, we do not notice the danger we are drifting into.

The church that has not wondered, and encouraged mankind to wonder, must be roused and hear the Lord's rebuke, "Could you not watch with me one hour?" (Matt 26:40). The church must keep awake, and "watch and pray" (Matt 26:41); that is, it must look out for the forces that are threatening our society with disintegration and it must watch them so they keep their distance. It must appeal to our rulers and to God to defend us from these dangers. It must overcome its distrust of the tradition it has absorbed from the culture around it, which have induced it to lower its guard. Our society assumes that the issues that face us have never been met before and Christians are always under pressure to make the same assumption. The church has to remind us how many times we have faced them before, and that the dignity of mankind therefore depends on our vigilance.

We have to know our own history, and so learn from the saints and teachers of the church. Unless we do this, we are subject to another clergy, the apparatchiks who lead the technologization of our relationships and attempt to mediate between us. These may have started as the clergy of the church, but they become ideologues of other systems. The church undergoes periodic convulsions in order to rid itself of these. The Reformation was the most painful of these episodes, in which layers of administrators and experts were cut out of the Christian body. The church always has to recover the truth that our lives cannot be parceled up and different functions delegated to such mediators. Every Christian, and all Christians together, are commissioned to wonder and pray and be the indivisible body of Christ in the world. No responsibilities can be entirely delegated away from the individual Christian, because Christ cannot be divided. All the offices of Christ and gifts of the Spirit are exercised by the whole body and in varying degrees by every member of it.

The clergy that lives from the Scripture and tradition of the church holds out the truth of mankind. We celebrate this truth and point to the prospects and hope of mankind. The university, having given up on unitary discourse about mankind, can only break mankind up into smaller pieces, to examine each in detached incomprehension and make its technological interventions. But what the university and the humanities have broken up, the church unites and holds together. The church that lives from the Scriptures is guardian of the unity and integrity of humanity.

The clergy cannot let the university be the criterion of its knowledge or the exclusive guard of the resources of the church's memory and identity. Only the worship of the whole church gives our ministers the whole gospel. The church must recover its confidence in its own teaching and be content to let the university go its own way. The church does not need the approval of the university, and the church's teaching certainly needs no certification from the education department. To recover its own teaching the church must cease to defer to the state on what can be taught.

The people of God cannot, and do not, surrender their responsibilities in this manner. They pass them on, but they do not give them away so that they are no longer exercised by the church. It is the impulse to delegate that creates new ranks of mediators and agents who wish to take all decision-making away from us. The worship of the church cannot be devolved into ethics and separate campaigns identified with justice and equality, for then the truth claims of Christian worship are not heard, and our worship has only a sentimental or aesthetic significance. The church is the only body that holds together the unity of mankind in Christ and thus holds the unity, the coherence and meaning, of all these otherwise separate issues. The whole unity of mankind, the whole identity and mystery of mankind, is in that cup that we may receive in the eucharist and that cannot be separated from it.

The gospel is the source of intellectual renewal. The church that hears the word of God must enable its ministers to remain obedient to that word. We have to intercede with our clergy and beg them to take our needs seriously. In our prayers we may remind them that they are appointed to pass this word on to us and need no permission from other authorities to do so. Let us encourage them to lead and teach and train us in the whole discipleship of Christ. Since the wonder that brings knowledge comes from the eucharist, the church must pass on the whole loaf.

3. SINGING — THE CHURCH BLESSES

God brings us into communion, with him and with all his people. The church is the form this communion takes on earth. God blesses and affirms mankind as good. God gives us this blessing to hold and to pass on so that we can affirm one another. In Christ, God brings the world into this communion, so God blesses the world by sending to it the body of Christ, opening the body for the world, and opening the world to the body. The church is brought into existence by the word and speech of God. By speaking to it and blessing it God sustains the church, and he blesses the world by sustaining the church as the true witness to this blessing. "Let us bless the Lord." "Thanks be to God."

The church is the blessing of God to the society to which it is sent. Christ serves us because he decides to, and in all his service of us he is entirely free. Since it is he who serves us, we are well-served and amply provided for: this is the basis of the Christian contribution to politics and the public square. The church speaks by blessing. Each Christian blesses and thanks each person for each gift, lesson, and reprimand. This blessing opens up a realm of public speech and public service.

Christ shares with us the self-control by which he is always free, even whilst he is our servant: he does not jostle for power as we do with one another. The assumption that we are left with less if God wields more power or responsibility is entirely untrue of God. God intends us to become like himself, self-controlled and so free to take our delight in one another and find service of one another its own reward. In his communion we are brought into relationships with all others and so may become catholic beings. Then we are free to receive and pass on the love and service, discipling and mutual correction, which is the form of his freedom.

Defending the Mystery of Mankind

Government is a set of forms within which we are able to make good judgments about public service and public well-being. We are not building a system: government cannot be a mechanism with an entirely known set of inputs and outputs. We are persons, which means there are too many unknowns for any mechanistic or technological approach to work. To assume total knowledge is to choose solutions that are totalitarian. A humble attitude to our political forms is the healthy one.

The church holds the secular liturgy up to question and affirms whatever it finds good. The church says that each particular human being is the most fundamental entity. Mankind is a mystery, by which is meant that he may be known, but he has to allow us to know him, and we can never know him utterly. He or she cannot be divided up and their responsibility devolved. Mankind without God doesn't know how to affirm this, with the result that we are tempted to transfer some of our individuality to the state, which then acts as though it were the most fundamental entity. The state cannot stop itself from attempting to master us. The church, with its strong account of our individual dignity, is therefore the defender of civil society against whatever state cannot remain modest.

God Satisfies Mankind

The Lord woos us. He does so with the gift of "his only begotten Son" (John 3:16). He has set the body of Christ on view everywhere before the world. Will the world be won over? The world can decide to be pleased by this gift and receive it as its passage into communion with God, and so as its salvation. Or the world can find the gift unpleasing and reject the Son and decide not to be propitiated by this body offered.

The Lord gives this body to the world as its way into its salvation. Christ keeps his body present, audible and visible to the world, preserving and renewing it, so the church can take the battering that the world endlessly metes out to it. God is wooing the world, and the body of Christ is the gift by which the world is wooed. The Lord seeks us, and having found us, calms us, treats our injuries, and removes the cause of our pain and distress. God is winning over the world by this patient offering of his Son. Since the Lord sets out to please us with this body, we can say that he hopes to propitiate us with it. God propitiates us.

We have seen that, when we do not identify the true God, we direct our love in all sorts of other directions and give ourselves away to whatever substitutes we invent. We have to be reoriented, our worship redirected, and we have to be purified. Christ purifies us by redirecting all our praise, from the many false directions in which we sent it, back to the Father. He gives us the love that purifies us of false loves and removes and expiates our sins, so that each of us may become as acceptable to each other as to God.

Christ purifies us. The church is made ready by Christ to be his body for the world. Since this purification happens in public, the church is continually humbled before the world, and we experience this as our passion. Christ performs this service and liturgy before the world in order to show, through his body, that this is the way that the world may take in order to enter communion with God.

Our Reasonable Sacrifice

The Spirit raises Christ for us and raises us into members of his body. Christ worships God for us. He speaks for us, supplies the words we need, so that we may participate in his worship, without limit and forever. As Saint Augustine puts it when he interprets Ps 85:1:

> The one sole savior of his body is our Lord Jesus Christ, the Son of God, who prays for us, prays in us, and is prayed to by us. He prays for us as our priest, he prays in us as our head, and is prayed to by us as our God. Accordingly, we must recognize our voices in him, and his accents in ourselves.[2]

Christ makes his body his "living sacrifice" (Rom 12:1). By "sacrifice," Augustine means worship, and by "living" he means live, ongoing, and uninterrupted. We are the sacrifice of Christ. He offers us to the world. He is the fire that purifies us from sin so that we endure forever. Since this fire burns off whatever does not belong to him, it always appears as though we are being consumed by it, and to the world it looks as though the church is being punished. This fire comes down from heaven, and the smoke that rises from the church in the form of our prayers ascends to God who receives it and is pleased by it. The prayers and worship of the people of God make a column of fire and cloud that unites earth to heaven and links each present time and place to the throne of God where all times and places are reconciled. The church is the firstfruits of the world-made-holy, now being held out to this generation for its inspection and approval.

In Christ the Spirit Glorifies Us

The Holy Spirit glorifies Christ. He distinguishes Christ from all others, and unites all others to him as members of his body. Christ cannot be isolated or separated from the whole people of God, whom he regards as his own glory. The Spirit sets us "in Christ." We know Jesus Christ (the one) as we acknowledge his people (the many), for he can only be known truly in this community that the Holy Spirit sanctifies. We come to know Christ through the life of the church, and so through all the saints and teachers whom the Holy Spirit presses into our service, along with the sacraments, tradition, gifts, and offices that enable us to participate in this worship.

The same Spirit who makes Christ unassailable enables his invincibility to serve us with an infinite patience and gentleness. Christ is the fundamental entity that cannot be broken up or reduced to anything else. He is the person who determines that we are persons and can never be reduced to objects. The Spirit raises you from me, making you more than I can ever control. Christ and the Spirit together are responsible for our unity and for all the distinctions that makes us different from one another. He differentiates us from one another, establishing us as unique and irreplaceable particulars.

Christ makes his people one indivisible whole, and the church is this future whole, making itself present to us in time. God sends us installments of this whole that make it publicly present within the world, in the communion of this people. The Holy Spirit holds the disparate community of the church together as this one body. He has glorified mankind and "crowned him with honor and glory" (1 Tim 1:17) in Christ. Since nothing can stop the Spirit who raised him from raising us, Christ's resurrection is promise and warning of our own. The church witnesses that the resurrection has commenced, in the resurrection of the one, Christ, and points ahead to its completion in the resurrection of the many.

In each place that it meets, the church is the evidence that Christ is drawing all of us to himself, bringing each into connection with all. This future and final assembly makes itself known to the present world in this hidden form of the church. In the eucharist each church intercedes with the Lord on behalf of its own locality. Each Christian prays for those members of his own family and society, past and present, and in these prayers these persons become present within the assembly.

Christ will bring us face to face with all men. The resurrection that raises us to God will also raise us to them, and them to us. Our Lord now sends us all these people ahead of him to us, so we receive him as we learn to receive them. Our resurrection, imperceptibly initiated at our baptism, presently comes to us in this slow anticipatory way through meeting these saints who already make up the glorified body of Christ. The eucharist, which is the union of God with man taking place before us, is gathering us and making us fully present and available to one another at last.

The Heavenly Liturgy and the Liturgy of This World

In its worship of God, the church examines itself to see whether our public witness is faithful, and whether the world can hear and see it. If we do not sing along with the first liturgy, that of Christ, it is because we are borne along by the second, the liturgy of the world that aims to get along without Christ. But we must also say that this second, worldly, liturgy is entirely dependent on the divine liturgy. The world that wants to put as much distance between itself and Christ as it can is able to do so only because Christ sustains its freedom to do so. Christ is the guarantor of the secular sphere and of our freedom to do without him for as long as we can.

The divine liturgy, which we experience as the worship of the church, sustains the secular liturgy of this world. The church makes this distinction between church and secular. This distinction does not divide the church from the world, but indicates that Christ has made himself the servant of the world and that we may participate in his service to it. All the activity of the church is just a particular expression of the liturgy of Christ. This action is his and ours only in the Holy Spirit, who glorifies him, and in him, glorifies us.

This worship and liturgy generate all our public activity. The church understands the days of the week as ways in which the fullness of Sunday spells itself out to us. Sunday is too much to take in all at once, so the day of resurrection spells itself out to us slowly, as Monday, Tuesday, and all the days in which we encounter the saints and, under their supervision, encounter the world. This service of Christian worship makes this distinction between Sunday and the days of the week, and between liturgy and secularity, and between the ordained Christian withdrawn from the world and the lay Christian sent into the world.

The Church as Image and Artwork

Everything going on in church is a revelation of Christ's service to us in gathering mankind. Everything that we sing is commentary on this service of his. The liturgy of the church is the communal body language of the church seen over the long term. Christian worship is a passion play, a public drama performed for the world first to watch and increasingly to participate in.

Every human being is the artwork of God and the very figure of God (*imago dei*) for us. When we are altogether assembled around Christ, it will become clear that all mankind is this artwork. The church displays images of some of the sanctified Christians of previous generations. We defer to these saints and even love them, because they have been given to us to be our pattern, so that we may become that image ourselves. Religious art is bad when it fails to let our gaze pass through it to these saints, and through them to Christ. Secular and modern kitsch derives from religious art that does not allow our gaze to pass through to this holy reality. Just as all human doing and making derives from God's work and service for us, so all human constructions are good as they allow themselves to be received with thanksgiving as gifts that point to whatever is beautiful, and bad as they fail to do so. The secular liturgy and art and labor are entirely dependent on the gift to mankind of participation in this divine liturgy. Our songs are derived from the songs of Christ to mankind, and our many loves are expressions of his one love for us. This true worship opens up the right way to live, and it cleanses us from all lesser ways. All popular song, with its language of love, and even all secular music with its rage against form, are derived from the songs of the church that communicate Christ's love for us. The world that wants to puts as much distance between itself and Christ as it can, and receive the love, or the memory of the love, without the giver of that love, can do so because Christ sustains its freedom to do this. Christ is the guarantor of the secularity of the world, and so of the freedom of man to do without Christ for as long as he can.

4. PRAYING—THE PASSION OF THE CHURCH

Christ prays for us. His prayers are heard by the Father. The church intercedes for the world, goes through the passion the world inflicts on it, and accompanies the world as it inflicts this passion on itself.

Christ speaks up for us before all others. He has interceded for us with those who were enraged at us, and speaks on our behalf to persuade them to be patient with us. Christ intercedes with us on behalf of those with whom we are at enmity, or of whom we are oblivious. His prayer is directed to us, to persuade us to be merciful with each other. Christ represents us to those whom we have made our victims, asking them to give us more time and another chance to turn around. Christ unceasingly asks us to release those whom, in our fear and rage, we have taken into our grip. We may release them, and so we ourselves may be released. We are immobilized by the grasp we have on others. He persuades our creditors and all those whom we have hurt to forgive us and let us go. He asks us to speak and pray for everyone and to pass on the forgiveness that we ourselves have received.

The Incarnation of the Lord

The church looks forward. We look back to the incarnation in order to see forward to Jesus and our own future with him. The communion of God spans past and future and brings all ages together into one. Christ makes man eternally and steadily incarnate and present to God. Christ is mankind with God, so that humanity is with God, never without him. As he is mankind with God, so he is person to person with us. In this holy communion he is entirely committed to us and makes himself available and vulnerable to us so that nothing has power to terminate this relationship.

Mankind is made for the society of God. We are created to be as free for God and for one another as God is free for us. In baptism we receive the divinity and humanity of God together, inseparably. We do not discover first the humanity of God and then the divinity, or discover the passion and then the resurrection. The resurrection demonstrates the indissoluble union of the Son with the Father, and the Spirit brings us into this same union. The resurrection comes to us, slowly so that we are unaware of it. It allows the wear and tear of the world to strip all false relationships from us. "We do not want to be unclothed" (2 Cor 5:4), says Saint Paul, but we look forward to being properly clothed at last. To put on glory is to take off sin. Since we experience the removal of sin as a passion, this passion is the form the resurrection presently takes for us.

All humanity is present to Christ. He is the truth of mankind with God. But we are not yet able to receive this full and complete incarnation, so he is not yet with us in the way he will be. We are present and incarnate to one another only in a very deficient way. Even when directly before you, I fail to receive all of what you want to communicate to me; I do not have the concentration to respond to you in anything like the way you would like. I do not honor or respect you as you should be honored, and I do not serve you as you should be served. I am afraid, so I withhold myself from you and do not let you become truly present to me, or let myself become truly present to you. Both inadvertently and deliberately we withhold ourselves from one another. Our human commonality is *fallen* flesh, a failure to be truly present and available to one another. In order to become properly incarnate to one another and to the Lord, we have to let go of whatever relationships are not right, and so we have a passion to undergo.

The Passion of Christ

The way of Jesus Christ is the way in which we may become fully present and incarnate to one another.

The way of Jesus is the passion. "We call to mind his death on the cross." We need to say three things about the passion: first, it is ours; second, it is Christ's; and, third, it is ours-in-Christ.

First, the passion is ours. We suffer and we inflict suffering on one another. We are thumped and helplessly we thump back, repeating and passing on the sin and passion we experience. In this way we suffer our passion pointlessly, without hope of reaching our goal when our suffering comes to an end. The whole creation labors and groans (Rom 8:22). The world that does not recognize Christ is always leaching and dissolving away. But Christ regards the world as his own people and his own body, so he understands their suffering as his own. He identifies himself with it entirely. The world is the body that belongs to Christ, and yet it pointlessly wounds itself and bleeds. The world does so because it does not yet recognize itself as Christ recognizes it; since it does not recognize him, it does not recognize itself as his, and so it does not know itself. As a result, it is in agony. The crucifixion displays the agony of the world. Only when it is publicly taken on, and undergone, by Christ, does this agonizing self-harming of the world come to an end.

Secondly, Christ takes on this suffering and makes it his own. He becomes incarnate in the world: his entire incarnation was a passion. In becoming a man, one among many, he took on all the mundane trials and experiences that we go through. We learn through some of these experiences, and fail to learn through others, but Christ learned through all the painful experiences and encounters. He served the same apprenticeship we all do but, unlike the rest of us, he did not resent it, or try to escape it, but suffered it contentedly and fully. He took what we try to evade. He received what was inflicted on him but, unlike the rest of us, he did not pass this punishment on. We lash out, but he did not. We attempted to force him into the same forms of evasion, expecting him to make his peace through compromise with the various forces around us. As he did not acknowledge any of these forces, our attempts did not succeed. So, we attempted to deny him life altogether. But he bore what, in our distress and rage, we meted out to him.

Christ's passion is the human passion, not evaded, not passed on, but fully experienced and suffered right to the end and so concluded.

He is able to bear us and is entirely content and free as he does so. In his passion he took on the full fury of human anguish. The anger of the world was directed at him, but he did not buckle but withstood everything we threw at him. It was uniquely directed at him and he absorbed it, until it was exhausted and finished. Although death took hold of Christ, death did not survive the encounter. It was finally unable to separate us from him. Those who are now in communion with him will never be separated from him or one another. Christ is with us, without limit and without end.

Our determination to take life away from him was outmatched by his ability to take the beating and stripping we gave him and to grow up through it into the true form of mankind. He used our violence for his up-building. Since he suffered what we inflicted on him, purposefully and effectively, and arrived at the true form of humanity, this passion turns out to be entirely purposeful.

So, thirdly, in the body of Christ, and therefore inseparably with Christ, we are now able to undergo this passion that strips all false and partial relationships from us. We suffer what the world inflicts on us. All the false relationships with which we have dressed ourselves up are taken away. Christ allows the world to strip us of these, so we lose everything that does not belong to us. And then he clothes us again, in the garments of the indissoluble new creation.

Our passion is therefore inseparably *his-and-ours* together. What the world gives so violently, the Holy Spirit enables us to receive purposefully. Christ's presence changes our passion from pointless and exhausting to purposeful and transformative. The Spirit directs our reception of this suffering so that we do not kick back and so pass the violence on; our suffering now brings the world into the communion of God. The body of Christ is the route opened by which the world may proceed to its redemption.

The Passion of Christ's Body in the World

In the passion Christ walks through the assembly of all mankind. Each of us is the storm he has to endure. We lash out and our blows rain down on him and he is pummeled and battered.

The Christ who is on the cross is us alone, as we wanted to be. But being without Christ has proved to be an agony to us. Without God, we inflict pain on one another and keep our whole society on the rack. We want to love and be loved, but we also fear that we may not be loved, and we want to remain in control, so we withdraw ourselves from love again. We are the cavity that sucks in love but does not let it out again. But Christ has drawn all our hate into himself, and he did not allow it to escape. Our fear is strong, but Christ is stronger and will prevail, and our fear will be overcome by his patience.

The cross is all the violence of the world distilled into one single moment. This violence becomes visible in this figure of Jesus crucified. The cross is both the appalling misery and violence that holds mankind, and the glory of God that even in all his misery holds on to mankind and sustains us. His covenant is irrevocable. Even if we attempted to destroy all creation, we could not destroy the love that creates it and that sustains every relationship in it. There is no place so appalling that God lets mankind go, so there is no place where evil will prevail and have the last word.

The cross is behind Christ, but it lies ahead for us. Our cross is not a repetition of his. Christ suffered alone, entirely without us, and indeed against us, since it was our aggression that he suffered. But in our passion, we are not alone, but with him. Since he cannot be separated from the Spirit, and by the Spirit we cannot be separated from him, our passion will not end in our destruction. Because we are joined to him our passion will not unravel us entirely. It will release us from what does not belong to us, so that we may finally be joined solely to him, and through him we will be truly joined to all others. We will be raised.

The passion is the way we may experience the resurrection now. We experience it as passion until the whole number comes in and the body is complete. Our course through life is a passage through the storm caused by the ungoverned forces, social, political, and natural that rage around us. The waves tower over us and close in on us so that we do not see how we will get through. They press in and try to break our self-possession. As soon as we are pushed out of our composure and give in to that rage, we become part of it. As Ps 124:1, 3–5 puts it: "If the Lord himself had not been on our side . . . they had swallowed us up quick, the waters had drowned us and the stream gone even over our soul." We must resist and absorb the violence of the storm and not pass its buffeting on. We must remain holy, still, and innocent.

Our entire Christian lives are this baptismal passage through this sea and through this narrow defile. All creation is disordered and frustrated. We inflicted this disorder on Christ and, now that we are in Christ, others inflict it on us. This storm of disorder must also pass through us, for we have to drink it down, and as we do, it will be pacified and come into its proper order.

It is no inanimate trouble that we have to go through but the deliberate resistance of the world, and the fury that other people now direct at us. We have to make our way through them. They try to prevent us passing, so we have to run the gauntlet of them. The world attempts to stop us coming through this dark passage with whatever thumps and kicks it can.

Christ takes us through our own passion. We ourselves have been part of that storm, for we were enemies of God who tried to oppose this body. The procession of God has had to proceed against our resistance. But as the end of the procession goes past, and our resistance to him is finally exhausted, we are caught up by Christ and join the procession of his people. Now we have become members of the procession that goes through the world; we attract the same rage that we once showed, but now we remain unmoved because untouched by it.

The Intercession of the Church

The gospel has come to us through the hands of many generations of Christians. They were not universally loved and thanked for this. Some of them were opposed and persecuted for their faithfulness to us and to other generations in the future. These saints suffered for the gospel for our sake. "All of these died in faith without having received the promises, but from a distance they saw and greeted them.... All these, though they were commended for their faith, did not receive what was promised, since God had provided something better so that they would not, apart from us, be made perfect" (Heb 11:13–40).

The whole church is an intercessory and priestly body. It prays and speaks up for the world. The world does not always celebrate with it. Christians pray for the world and the world relies on them to do so, delegating its own responsibility to the church. The church therefore appears loaded with sin, its appearance apparently entirely compromised. It is the sin of the world that the church carries, and is itself caught up in, and bearing accusation and ridicule is part of our priestly calling.

The church offers its high view of human identity and the confidence that comes from it renews civil society as a whole. The distinction between the church and the world is fundamental, yet it is a permanent source of aggravation. The church says that mankind is called by God and utterly restless until he heeds that call. He tries to distract himself from this restlessness by pursuing other goals, and yet no other goal provides the satisfaction and release that mankind seeks, and so he takes out his frustration on the church. As long as we are still restless it is because we are on the way to our redemption, regardless of whether we are at any moment moving backwards or forwards, we are unable to silence this call that keeps us in motion.

Christians suffer for the sake of the church. We continue the sufferings of Christ until they are vindicated and completed by the reconciliation of all. As the apostle Paul says, "I fill up in my flesh what is still lacking in Christ's afflictions for the sake of his body" (Col 1:24), so we are also "poured out like a drink offering" (2 Tim 4:6) and rejoice in this.

When we refer to Christ bleeding, we are referring to the Christians, and to the people of Israel, whose lives have been lived in service of which we are the beneficiaries. They became martyrs for our sake. Christ reckons them his, and so refers to them as his own body and blood. He considers their labor to be his own so when they are persecuted he is bleeding. To despise or persecute the saints is to "crucify the Son of Man all over again" (Heb 6:6).

The Church as Passageway for the World

The church is the way that has opened to us. With Christ, and directed and enabled by him, we may now open ourselves and let the world enter him through us. The church is the gate through which the world can enter Christ. The Lord commands the church to become this opening.

The church and the church's passion is the path along which the world must go. The world is saved by the service and passion of the church, the body of Christ. The church suffers because it takes whatever the world metes out in its fury. This generation of the people of God are the conduit through which this generation of the world may enter the communion of God. Thus, it is the church that is present, with Christ, in the eucharist.

5. EUCHARIST—THE ASCENSION OF MANKIND

In the eucharist we enter the holy communion of God and become truly present to each other. The spiritual bread from which all our materiality comes makes us embodied and steadily available to each other.

The Living Sacrifice

Sacrifice means worship. This worship starts in heaven, for it is the divine liturgy, which is the conversation of the Father, Son, and Spirit. As they are holy, so is their communion and conversation. Christ worships the Father, the Father adores the Son: their life is perfect and requires nothing beyond itself; it does not come into being, but is always in being, and all creatures receive their being from it.

In prayer Jesus is always with the Father, together and united, and so in an unending conversation. In the church we are caught up into this conversation, as it is made audible to us in the prayer and liturgy of Christ. Christ speaks and prays to the Father: through the resurrection their uninterruptible conversation and unbreakable communion has made themselves present within creation. The Son presents us to the Father, and thus we are his holy gifts, his sacrifices, and the demonstration of his good stewardship. He raises us continually to God, and as the Father receives us from him, our existence is affirmed.

Christ is *our* sacrifice in the sense that, in giving thanks to the Father for him, we lift him up in acknowledgment what we receive through him. We are able to lift him up in thanks and praise because he lifts us up in reality. We "sacrifice" Christ, with our thanks and praise, returning acknowledgment that it is he who holds us in communion with God and with each other. Augustine puts it this way:

> He is both the priest, himself making the offering, and the offering. This is the reality, and he intended the daily sacrifice of the Church, being the body which he is the Head, learns to offer itself through him. This is the true sacrifice.[3]

Behind Christ in the eucharist is the whole communion of saints. They wait for us. At the resurrection they will be revealed to us and we will be raised to them. When we can hear them perfectly, we will at last be made capable of seeing them. Meanwhile the Holy Spirit supplies us with all Christ's people, and all Christ's people supply us with his Spirit and all our future catholicity. They are in that cup, they are the secret of our future, and we will finally be ourselves when we are with them. Saint Augustine puts it like this:

> If, therefore, you are the Body of Christ and His members, your mystery is presented at the table of the Lord, you receive your mystery. To that which you are, you answer: "Amen." . . . Be a member of Christ's Body, so that your "Amen" may be the truth.[4]

Christ is at work. His service of the Father includes service to us. He is the ever-living sacrifice, the servant who serves and provides for his people, making them holy and giving them without limit what is his to give, which is his own uninterrupted life and communion with God and with all creation. His eternity with the Father empowers his service and enables him to be the eternal servant of mankind, entirely and inexhaustibly available for us.

Christ makes us holy and presents us as such, so we are *his* sacrifice. Christ the head *sacrifices his body*, that is, he makes it holy and then he presents it as holy to the Father. Christ is our holy-maker: he gives us his holiness and then gives us to God. In all this the gift is both one person, Christ, and many persons, all those whom he brings with him. Not only are the giver and receiver persons but so is the gift they give and receive from one another.

Being Made Holy

Christ makes his people holy. He brings us into the holy communion and life of God. Since we are being made holy, in this Christian sense, we have to say that *we are the sacrifice of Christ*. In the Old Testament books of Exodus and Leviticus we learn that in the temple sacrifices Israel demonstrated that God is purifying and forming his people. As evidence of this sanctification process, God commands the people of Israel to report back at intervals with samples of their husbandry. Chief evidence of this sanctification would be the health and moral maturity of the people themselves. The community of Israel brought animals to the temple for God to inspect and pronounce good (or not) and thus to assess and agree on the progress of this sanctification. It is the whole people that is being made holy: the animals and produce of the land are subordinately holy as they demonstrate and contribute to this process.

As we practice and learn, we present the Lord with the products that are evidence of our learning. We are to send him gifts. What we have to send up from God's inspection is ourselves. Yet we are not yet holy, not yet ready to go, so we send representatives and tokens of ourselves. We send someone else up, and send with them something that will represent us before the Lord. This could be whatever we have produced in our own household that will be truly a token of ourselves.

In its worship Israel spelled out that the prayers of the righteous and the fertility of the land are linked by its relationship with God. We are not driven by fear to placate God with gifts, but rather God adores us, woos us, and in everlasting patience serves us. All his creatures are his gifts, and they are made holy as he gives them to us.

Mankind as Receiver of the Gift

The question here is what is sacrificed, to which the answer must be given in terms not of *what* but of *whom*. Two things have to be said. Christ is person and Christ is thing; he is the giver and the gift, or rather, he is that stream of gifts by which he presently makes himself available to us. By them we are enabled to grow to maturity, are made holy, and are satisfied.

In Christ, God is given to mankind. But also, in Christ, mankind is really received by God: mankind is the gift that the Father accepts from the Son. The giver gives us gifts and is himself the gifts he gives, but he does not cease to be himself. The gifts are fully him, but he is never exhausted by them. He can give himself away in gifts without end, but he cannot finally be given away and so lost.

In Christ God has given a person. In the course of our refusal to receive him, we cut him off from life and so make him a mere dead thing. But God does not let him remain a thing, but raises him. Being a thing was something that Christ did for the three days of Easter to show that we cannot succeed in taking away the life that God gives. Ultimately this gift does not remain mute and unresponsive. God will not give up on us. The crucified body turned into the resurrected body, so revealing that Christ is not a dead thing, but an unchangeably living person. We did not overcome Christ or succeed in turning him finally into a corpse and a thing. He consented to suffer, so he is pierced, but only willingly, and not finally. We do not make him suffer, for he bears us in complete freedom.

The resurrection shows that the passion is free. The passion is the patient working of the resurrection on earth.

It is good to have available the person who can provide what is necessary at the right moment. They produce just what we need but do not have. We need our *daily* bread. God gives us the materiality that sustains us in life, in the form of the creatures we consume. But equally, although each gift is good, it is good only in that moment. It lasts a day; tomorrow we will be as needy as before. Thus, what we need is the regular *supply* and thus a *supplier*. We need both provision for today and the supplier who will give us ongoing provision, and so an open-ended perspective. Hope is the prospect of a future without a limit on it. Only this prospect of unlimited life, indefinitely and eternally renewed, gives meaning to the present existence of any living creature.

Christ is the one who serves us, without limit and forever, and thus he is irreducibly and eternally *person*. He is the priest who offers and gives this gift, and he is the one who accepts it and receives it. His priesthood is living and eternal.

Christian Sacrifice and Pagan Sacrifice

We said that the Christian account is different from the pagan account of sacrifice. Sacrifice does not primarily mean to kill or to give away but *to make holy*. The very etymology of the word "sacrifice" points us in this direction—*sacri-* (holy) *ficere* (to make). Along with "sacrament" and "sanctification," "sacrifice" refers to work of the persons of God that makes us holy and members of their holy communion.

This means that the church's use of the term "sacrifice" is not at all what may normally be meant by that word. By this term, our society means a death. By the same term, the church means life that is holy and therefore inextinguishable; it refers to what does not die and cannot die. These are two violently opposite senses of the same word.

In common usage, sacrifice is a coerced exchange, an exchange in a finite economy, in which I have to offer you something if I want something from you. Something is given up in order to gain something else. Something is killed so that other lives can be saved, or that life is even the punishment and penalty sought as reparation by some power terrible enough to enforce such a demand.

But when we address each other as Christians, we mean something entirely different. We simply have to explain, with reference to Scripture, what this different sense is. We need to ensure that our account of sacrifice is shaped by the whole narrative of Scripture. This requires that we discuss who *receives* this gift; at different moments in the evangelical narrative this is variously the world, the church and God. Since this is Christian theology, it must always be theology of the whole Christ, never Christ without us, or us without Christ.

Our Sacrifice and Service in Christ

We may also raise and offer one another to God. We may present one another to God, as the Spirit enables us to do so. Now we can say also that other people are our sacrifice and offering. We bring them to God. We bring the people who owe their faith to us into the body of Christ. The gift we bring to God in Christ is *one another*.

The Lord commands the church to open in order that the world may enter and begin its Passover. The church—the people of God present to us in this generation—is the long passageway along which the world must travel in order to enter the communion of God. They may lash out in rage at the Christians who line the route they have to take. But they will be able to absorb that rage without being moved by it, and without giving it back, and in this way the world will be saved through the witness, service, and endurance of the saints. Thus, it is the church, the body of Christ, which is present, with Christ, in the eucharist. The whole church is given to the present church, and the present church is part of the eucharistic bread that it holds out to the world.

We are the many fragments that Christ has gathered up. He holds out to us the one bread that is us-with-him. Christ is in that eucharistic cup, and we and all creation are in there with him. "There you are on the table, there you are in the cup," as St Augustine says.[5] "If you receive them well, you are that which you receive."[6]

We are Christ's sacrifice and offering, and Christ is our sacrifice and offering. "This sacrifice is ourselves. . . . Such is the Christian sacrifice: the multitude—a single body in Christ."[7] In the Holy Spirit, Christ makes us present to one another. He does not do this unilaterally, for this would be an imposition. He offers us one another, and he waits until we receive one another, because we are ready and willing to do so. Christ not only gives but also waits for us to receive what he gives. He does not give us one another all at once, but serially, through time. He serves us and waits for us; Christ's waiting is what time is. For now, Christ makes himself present only in this disguised form, so that our freedom to receive this life from him, or not to receive it, is entirely ours.

The resurrection that raises us to Christ will also raise us and bring us face to face with all people. He now sends us all these people ahead of him to us, so we are already meeting these saints who already make up his glorious body. Because Christ is with the Holy Spirit in that cup, the saints, their whole sanctified people, are in that cup. As he comes to us, Christ brings all men and women with him, and when we can receive them all and can give thanks to him for them the incarnation of all creation in Christ will be complete.

Body and Blood

True worship and pure sacrifice, praise and thanksgiving start in heaven. Or rather, they are what heaven is. Heaven is reality at full tilt. Earth is that same reality slowed right down for us. This worship is truth unlimited—the truth of God delivering the truth of mankind. This divine liturgy prays and speaks truly, and it does not become any less truthful when it allows us to participate in its truth.

Christian worship is always embodied. There is a proper materiality to our sacrifice of thanks and praise. Christians say that creation, and every creature embodied within it, is good. Pagans are not so sure.

Our praise and thanks do not become more crassly material and less rational or spiritual when it is accompanied by the action of our bodies in standing, kneeling, signing ourselves with the cross. There are many modes in which human bodies communicate. All our actions and relationships are embodied, and our prayers are embodied prayers. We cannot be persons without bodies, for our bodies are forms of presence to others. It is for other people's benefit that we have bodies, for only so can they find us and be able to address us.

Towards the end of the eucharist we pray: "We thank you for feeding us with the body and blood of your Son." This comes from the Gospel of John: "Unless you eat the flesh of the Son of Man and drink his blood you have no life in you . . . he who eats my flesh and drinks my blood abides in me and I in him" (John 6:53–56).

Christ gives us his *body*. In case we found that too easy to get down, he also gives us his blood. "Unless you eat my body and drink my blood you shall have no part in me" (John 6:53). This was the teaching that repulsed pagans of the Roman regime of the first three centuries and was the basis of the charge for which many Christians were martyred. And left on its own, this very gnomic statement continues to baffle and offend.

"Body" and "blood" are not self-explanatory. They are metonymies and we have to find synonyms for them. We do not *replace* the words "body" and "blood" with such synonyms but simply use them in addition any time we are asked to explain what we mean. Let us look at these. In each case we find that they are metonymies of the *resurrection* as well as of the crucifixion.

This body appears to be this inert object, the eucharistic bread. But the bread is simply to direct our attention to the body of Christ that is present and the body of Christ that is still absent and to come. Its presence is not complete, but it points ahead to the future redemption, the eschaton, and so we have to confess this present *absence*. Until the evangelical narrative is spelled out and our attention is drawn to the body of Christ and the priesthood of the whole Christ, this bread will remain just a puzzlingly inert object.

But Christ is the *bread of life*, the living and indivisible one, whom nothing in creation can stop, break, or make their object. The world is simply a chaos of inert objects without meaning until the arrival of one who is life himself. He gives them life, and in giving life to us he turns us from things into persons, from dead to living, from dumb materiality to free and vocal beings.

Christ is the bread of life, the single indivisible loaf that nothing in creation can divide. God has collected us from all corners of the world and by his almighty power combined these fragments into this single entity. The loaf raised and displayed at the altar is the reconciliation of all things and so the first batch of the new creation.

Then Christ, the loaf, breaks himself open for us and shares himself with us. The indivisible divides and distributes himself. Since wheat is harvested and milled, bread represents something broken. Bread means unity as much as it means division and passion. "He who eats my flesh and drinks my blood abides in me and I in him" (John 6:53–56). We have said that "eats" (*trogein*) has the sense of bite and chew, as though we should grasp him with both hands, sink our teeth into him, and not let go. He has fastened us to himself, so we should fasten ourselves to him and cling on. He tells us to get our teeth into him and into no one else. We are not to grab, bite, or consume anyone else. He alone is able to take the force of our desperation. He alone can be constantly consumed and yet remain untouched. We cannot break him. Only he is impregnable and indivisible and so can withstand what we inflict. He can supply us endlessly, and as we receive our supplies from him, we are able to release all those whom we have seized and have been consuming and let them go free. His command to "eat him" means that we should sink our teeth into him and into no other human being. Any creature can be destroyed by our aggression, but Christ we will never destroy, but may live from eternally.

We are offered the cup with the words "The blood of Christ, given for you."

The indivisible and impassible Christ tells us that he bleeds when his people bleed. The saints who came before us poured their lives out to bring this gospel. Since they are Christ's, he regards their blood as his. We are being lifted to God by the saints who came before us; they have worked for us and suffered to bring the gospel to us, built this church, composed these hymns, taught us these Scriptures, and put up with our contempt. They passed Christ to us, and we may say that they continue to lift us up to God and to be the service of Christ for us, even to have become Christ for us: blood is the passion of the body, and in this context "blood" signifies the suffering and bleeding of that body. The pagan world drinks this cup in one sense: it consumes and destroy Christ's saints. We drink this cup in the other sense: we take the rage and resistance of the world and drink it down, so take on the suffering of the world which Christ has now made his sufferings. Then this is our blood which, with that of all the saints, flows for the healing of the nations.

But the blood is also resurrection. "Blood" means "of one blood," so referring to people who are members of one family: the same blood runs in their veins. When the Son enters the most holy place it is by his own blood, the royal blood that is in his veins, for he is a member of that family and household, for he is the Son of the Father. We are made members of the household of God, brought into one circulation with him, so his life courses from him to us, and around our bodies locking us into one metabolism with him. Thus, blood is victory, resurrection, and unity quite as much as it is passion and division.

The infinitely diffusible wine is the many who are one because the circulation of this blood and life makes this body one. In this part of the account, we represent no loss of blood for him, and so no bleeding out into an uncontrolled damaging dissolution. Now "blood" refers to the Spirit who runs from Christ to his body, filling and animating that body, and running back from it to its head and source again, sustaining us in a single circulation with him. Here this is blood understood as unity, not as loss. The bread and wine refer both to division and death, and they refer to Christ's unity and resurrection. It is this indissoluble unity, with God in the Spirit, that makes it possible for him to give himself to us and so to suffer and to die in order to bring us into this communion in which we can never die.

The Whole Christ and the Eucharist

If we assume that "Christ" only ever means Christ in isolation, without the company that is his glory, we will be unable to give a proper account of the eucharist. We have to say that Jesus is glorified as *Christ*. The Father has glorified him by adding these people to him, making him their king, and making them his people. They are his glory. His body, which is his presence for us, includes them. If we want to receive him, we also have to receive them. The name and title "Christ" always means Christ together with his people, Christ-and-his-body. He is entirely himself, and simultaneously he is with us and we with him. The relationship he has with us never confuses, reduces, or threatens his identity. All our existence comes from him to us: nothing from our existence washes back to make him less than he is, the eternal Son.

The problem comes when we understand Christ as he appears on the cross only, cut off from God and from mankind. Christians may no longer know him as he seemed to be on the cross, apparently rejected, condemned, reviled, alone, and utterly without support. Now it is clear that he has not been abandoned, and we can conclude that the cross was not at all the event we thought it was. He always had the glory that his Father gave him, so was always accompanied and supported. Now he is always fully able to support us and sustain us in his good company, so the glory he receives from the Father, he shares with us.

Then we can set out this eucharist as act of the glorified Christ, the unity of Christ with his people, the head of the body. He is both head and body: we are body dependently, when he is head. We do not make him head by being his body. Our "embodiedness" and our "bodiliness" are entirely a function of his. It is he who "bodies" us. Each of us is a member of his body, and affirms our body as the proper embodiment of our person, by his willingness to be our Head. We are what we are because he gives us his acknowledgment and approval.

Each of us, and all of us together, are the embodiment of Christ in creation, and so in nature. Nature is then embodied by us. Christ commands creation to serve us by giving us the bodies by which we can come together, share life with each other and so become human. All our identity comes from Christ, and remains true as we acknowledge this and return our thanks to him, naming him as our head and our Lord. All our bodies are products of creation. Yet it is not creation that makes them what they are, but Christ who gives them and maintains them in order that we can be present and available to one another. Creation gives us the bodies by which we can locate one another, because Christ commands it to do so.

Take, Eat, This Is My Body

In the pagan understanding, where the strong take from the weak, "eating" implies that you take something from someone without their consent, and eat it without them. Eating means "taking away from," which means that you are a predator.

In the Christian version, "eating" means "eating together," sitting in a circle or around a table. By eating together, everyone a willing participant, we become equals. The provider of this food is senior to us but, since he eats with us, he considers us his equals.

In the Gospel of John, Christ tells his people to grasp him and sink their teeth into him (John 6:53–6). He commands us to act as though we were the predators and he was our prey. Obviously, we who once took him by force, now clearly have no power over him, but since he commands us, Christ gives us that authority and power. He gives himself, opens himself to us, and lets us in so we can take what we need from him and hold on to him.

In repeating the Lord's words, "This is my body, eat me," Christians are offering an abbreviation of this teaching. But it is never enough to offer the abbreviation, assume that its meaning is obvious and the rest can be deduced. When this is all people learn, they are baffled, and some, attempting to put the pieces together for themselves, are repelled by the suggestion of literal flesh-eating that appears. It is clear from Eusebius's

History of the Church that the garbled version of Christian teaching that the pagan authorities heard, or perhaps pretended to hear, was that Christians were commending the eating of human flesh, and with at least the appearance of moral indignation, tried to stamp this faith out, and this either drove, or excused, two great persecutions under Decian and Diocletian.

In the pagan version, which represents life in the natural world, eating is about snatching, pulling, tearing, and holding on. Taking and dividing are what human beings most fundamentally do. We go into the field or vegetable garden, cut plants and eat them. We tear these plants out of the soil, bring them in, cut them up again and divide them among everyone around the table. Or, if we are stuck in the animal world, which is the world as pagans know it, we gain our food by snatching from other weaker people. We may justify this by calling them slaves, so that it seems natural. On the pagan definition, this is what human beings do to each other. We take them and we break them.

For Christians, there is another sense of taking what creation has grown for us which is fundamental to our being human together. We provide for one another, and this means that we plant and harvest, for ourselves and for one another. All humans are always engaged in taking and dividing up what creation provides. We live by harvesting by tearing or cutting whatever we have either planted or found. We take, divide, and distribute. Force is obviously involved when we harvest animals, less so when we are harvesting crops. Christ is showing us that we are not bound, by necessity, death, or any dark force, to grab and divide. We are not bound to harvest what other people have planted, seize whatever they have worked for, or, making them our slaves, drive them to work for us until they drop dead of exhaustion. We do not have to "consume" them. We all understand that, if you work them too hard, or take everything away from people, leaving them with nothing, you will be responsible for their death. You haven't actually eaten them, but morally you have expended and consumed them.

We are no longer bound to act in the same way as predatory beasts. The beasts are bound to this life of catch-and-kill before you are caught and killed. Nature does not force us to be predatory because Christ has freed us from the compulsions of nature. He has seized us and carried us out of its power so we, though always formed by nature, are now bound by freedom. We are no longer compelled to rob people or work them to death. We longer have to chew other people up and gulp them down.

We are not obliged to take by force, or rob or kill in order to eat. We can grasp Christ, hold on to him, and take from him, and he will never be exhausted. He instructs us to do so. He commands us to grasp him only, and ceaselessly take our sustenance from him. He is the only animal that we can feed on without killing, because he is the only animal we can never kill. He is the eternal body, and his eternity will give life to our mortal bodies as long as we take and eat what he gives us. These plant and animal bodies are the provision of Christ to us, all intended to bring us to maturity and sustain us in eternity. Of all the creatures that could provide human sustenance, just wheat, the vine, and the olive are singled out to be representative of the rest, so only bread, wine, and oil are set before us when we are gathered as his body.

This account relies on understanding that human life is about taking and dividing, with various degrees of consent and force. When what people have worked for is taken from them, and even more when they themselves are taken into slavery, we may say that we have consumed them. Christ has taken us and freed us from the compulsion to consume one another. But he commands us to grasp him and hold onto him with all the force of which we are capable. He tells us to bite down on him. For as long as we keep our teeth and fingers sunk into him, and only him, we will be secure and will be provided for. He will bring us to our proper destination, which is life in his community, with him, with all members of his company and with all the creation he has redeemed. This is the body that grows from this head, and which receives its whole definition from him.

No account of the eucharist is adequate until it includes an explanation along these lines. It must contrast our pagan and animal life with the new life that Christ has opened to us, by which we stop consuming each other but allow ourselves to be held and nourished by him. Christ orders creation so that it sustains us mortals as members of his body eternally.

6. WHOLE PEOPLE — GLORIFIED BY GOD

The Christian service of worship is Christ's service. It is his worship of God, and his service to us, by which he brings us into his worship of God. He makes us holy and presents us as holy to God who receives us so. He brings mankind into existence, makes him perfect, and unites mankind with God. We will be with God, and so "with angels and archangels and with all the company of heaven."

The Church Is Vindicated

The church is the assembly made up of all the members of Christ, both those who, for us, are in the past and in the future. They want us to join them and take up our places with them. This assembly, which is future to us, will make itself known to the present world in Christ and in the Spirit, all at once, at the judgment. In the incarnation we have a preview of this coming together of all things. This future assembly makes itself present to us now, little by little, as his incarnation is continually set before us in every eucharist. In it we are increasingly clothed with his glorious body and become increasingly bodily available to one another. This assembly includes the leaders of all nations called together here to give an account of themselves before the world and before God.

Christ Is the Truth of Mankind

God sustains and prepares his people. He brings us and all creation into being and now makes us holy. He invests us with his undying life. We see Christ because he has taken on our created materiality, and we see him as our Lord and God because his life is redeeming this materiality and making it glorious. "Thou within the veil has entered, thou on earth both priest and victim in the eucharistic feast," according to the hymn by Chatterton Dix. "Our great High Priest" is "veiled" and "robed in flesh." God became present and incarnate to us in Jesus Christ. The purpose of this incarnation was that we be perfectly present and incarnate to him and to one another. As he comes to us, Christ brings everyone with him, and when we can receive them all and can give thanks to him for them, the incarnation of all creation in Christ will be complete. We look forward to becoming properly present to one another and this is what our hope of the resurrection is.

Jesus's incarnation and passion are the work of his eternity, which we know as the resurrection. His eternity, his inexhaustible economy, allows him to become present to us, and so present in time. And his eternity brings creation into being and so creates time just so we may come into communion with him, and receive his presence and receive one another from him, so we will be human as he is already perfectly human.

The eucharist is both the passion of Christ and the resurrection and ascension of Christ. But both passion and resurrection point forward to what is to come. The crucifixion is about the division and pain of the world, but it is also this pain brought to an end and this self-rending reversed, and mankind saved from this passion and redeemed through it. The resurrection of Jesus is how we gain some foretaste of *our own* resurrection, and so of the eschaton. The Eucharist is both the passion of all mankind, and the resurrection and ascension of all mankind in Christ.

Christ sits at the right hand of the Father. In him we become mankind-with-God, and in the communion of God each of us becomes united to all humanity. Christ is all mankind, raised from the dead to eternal life in communion with God. He is therefore the whole colossal future of humankind, making itself gently present to us here and now so that we decide whether we will admit it and want to be part of it. It asks us whether we will allow it to come into being.

Christ is risen and ascended with his whole people and glory. He is not available to us as the single individuated body of Christ. Joined to him, they are the body we refer to when we talk about the presence of Christ: the body or presence of Christ refers to Christ accompanied by his whole people, and so to him as he is now inseparable from this glorious company.

Yet the body of Christ is not yet complete, and the presence of Christ is not yet apparent to us. It cannot be complete without the full complement of his people and thus without the very last member of that body. The humble must take up their place in the body before Christ is all in all. If the humble are left out this is a false and idolatrous "totality," partial, and therefore not built to last. Only when the full number are in and the body is complete, will Christ be everywhere publicly all in all. Then the kingdom will be complete, and the king of that kingdom will be recognizable to us at last.

Mankind is a mystery that cannot be controlled. It is not just our present, defined by the limits of our imagination, but our future that God has at heart here. God is guardian of our freedom, and he will not let us give it away. We wrestle unceasingly with the question of our identity. Perhaps we would rather creep into a dark corner or even bring about our own extinction than continue to wrestle with the dark shape of our own future.

God seeks us. He does so for our sake, not for his. If Christ believes that we are worth going out to search for, we are indeed so. If he is finally there to receive us, then we will finally have life. Since there are no constraints on him, or on his ability to pull us together and sustain us in being, we will have life without limit or end. Because he is truly himself, independent of any relationship he has with us, he is able to give us the recognition that establishes us. Only the Father can recognize who the Son brings home, and call them by name with enough authority finally to settle who they are. "While he was still a long way off, his father saw him and, filled with compassion, ran to him" (Luke 15:20). If God comes and receives us, we live indeed. If he comes to gather the dead, this must mean that they are living, and not dead at all. The Holy Spirit brings us together in Christ to recognize the Father, and so to say that he, and no other, is the one who can do this.

Christ has the power to make the persons of our past, the persons of our future. The resurrection of the dead is a transfer out of the past to life without confinement, unlimited and eternal. Christ with the Spirit gives us a place in the communion of saints. Each person, in particular each saint, brings us some part of this good gift of God to us, and with it some part of our very own identity.

Though we may all be situated in history, in-turned, dead to one another, we are not trapped in it, for we are not out of earshot of the call of God; we will be raised and brought to face one another, both with those we wanted to avoid, and those we assumed were dead and gone and could not be raised. Nothing in all creation has the power to remain dead before God. We will yet become human, for with much more patience that we can imagine, our resurrection is waiting for us. "He is able to keep us from falling, and to present us faultless before the presence of his glory with exceeding joy" (Jude 24).

Christ is drawing us up into life in this communion. God always intended to come to mankind and stay with us, and that in the course of this coming we would grow up, and this process is delayed, but not halted, by our fear and rebellion. Saint Irenaeus says that man begins as an infant and so an innocent, who is called up into maturity in God's communion; in order to grow, we have to undergo an apprenticeship. Christ is the one who has undergone this apprenticeship to the end. He is now the mature and completed form of man.

In Christ man ascends into this communion, and this ascension is the whole narrative of God with man. *Coming-into-*communion with

God is the way that we *are* in communion with God. We should use the term "ascension" to cover the whole narrative of God with us, and sanctification is the mode in which we exist in this communion—in it we are always being made holy. This process of our formation and transformation process is the ascension of man to God.

The Consummation of Creation

Man is glorified in Christ. He is the material creature who comes into free relation with all material creation. All material creation becomes his body. And man becomes the whole man—Christ. Thus, all material creation becomes the body of Christ. It is this body because Christ is its head. The head supplies life and form and substance to the body. And by this body of creation, and these bodies of other people, we gain the life and substance by which we can be present to each other and recognize each other as the body of which Christ is the head. It is for us that Christ has this material body. He swathes himself in creation, for us (Ps 104:1). Christ makes himself a creature and so a single item within creation for us, and he makes himself many things and provisions—for us. The human race contains within it the whole world: all things in the world will make up the body of Christ. Through humanity all creation will participate in the freedom that comes with life with God. As man is raised, so creation is raised, and becomes free.

Man is being dressed in glory. We expect the faces of those around us in the worship to shine. When we are gathered to worship, we see the Christian who stands in front of us, for whom the traditional term is "bishop," as the image of how we will be, redeemed and made glorious. He shines with the glory that will be common to us all, though this glory may only be apparent those who are themselves being transformed. We are being dressed in Christ, and thus dressed in the whole glorious company of Christ. The book of Leviticus tells us that when this high priest comes into the holy place "He shall put on the holy linen tunic, and shall have the linen undergarments next to his body, fasten the linen sash, and wear the linen turban; these are the holy vestments" (Lev 16:4). Christ now serves us by stripping and separating us from all that does not belong to us. Christ takes one set of clothes off to dress us in another.

Christ is dressed in all creation. How else should we, who are material, see him? We are material, and we can see and perceive whatever is material. We have seen that each of the bodies which make us visible and present to one another, constituted of all the plant and animal bodies we consume, is itself a gathering of the material elements of creation. For us therefore Christ is dressed in material creation. The redeemed and glorified world will provide the body of Christ in the form we can receive it. All things in the world will make up the body of Christ and so Christ's people will embody creation. Each of us embodies a particular part of the earth, so creation lives in each human body. Creation lives in and through us, just as much as we live in it. We could even say that creation exists as the body of each member of Christ's assembly. In Christ we are the "person" of creation, the indivisible unity that preserves creation immune from time and death. In the eucharist, material creation is able to sing the praises of God and so participate through us in the freedom of God.

Since Christ clothes himself with his people, in him all persons and all material creation are forever present with God. In his liturgy to God and service to us Christ unites all creation with God. This work of bringing these many into one is what is going on in the great eucharistic prayer of offering, the anaphora. For the benefit of world, the saints who are assembled behind Christ participate publicly in his office of raising and embodying the world to God. As Christ and his body speak for it and present it to God, creation's divisions disappear, there is reconciliation between the social and the natural worlds, and so we are able to live with, rather than against, the order of creation. As the eucharist is the reconciliation of mind and body, intellect and materiality, so the church is the union of nature in humanity and nature, and freedom come to creation.

Eternity Gives Us Time

This world is God's place for us. It is the house and temple in which he will live with us and us with him. All that is in it is good, and it remains good as we allow God to renew and refresh it for us. When we do not receive it from him and thank him for it in our worship, the world becomes disordered and we ourselves become increasingly desperate and at odds, and a danger to one another.

From the communion of God, eternity floods in to us, so that eternity renews time without end. Eternity is breaking into time, divinity, eternally breaking into humanity and making it holy. We experience this as an inbreaking into history; eternity breaks into humanity both eternally and historically. Worship services that seem to us to be set at different times are going on simultaneously, in the time God gives them, and so immediately before God. God supplies them with the time they have, and he supplies that undivided time to us, as we can take it, in small installments, one after another. Time originates with God. He supplies it to his people. It spills out from the church into the world outside the church, there to become the plain, linear, everyday time, that we assume is the only sort of time there is. Each church service is the merciful extension of new time for the world, an extension of opportunity to all its people.

The time which God came to mankind is both temporal (one moment in our time) and it is eternal, and so not limited to the past. To the question "when" we have to reply with all three tenses. He *came*, he *comes*, and *is now present* (by his Spirit) and he *will* come. In Christ the future of the whole human race has penetrated forward into our time. Christian hope means that we can see our future as free; it does not see past and future as opposed, but the future as the reordering and summation of the past in which none is lost. The present is sustained by installments of the future, which we may receive as invitations and summons to take up our place among the assembly of all free persons. The future is that large number of persons who wait for us ahead. Those now around us are the small advance party sent to us by the whole assembly that is waiting ahead of us. Eternity is coming to us now, live. It comes in the form of people, whom we must receive, which requires that we let go of all false relationships, and this means that we must wait for them until they freely let go of all false relationships, and receive us.

We see the future of humanity every time the Christian people is gathered. At the head of these people in church we see the person who is the figure of us with God, and God with us. There is one single human being, who is an image and icon of Christ. Christ puts him there just in order that we can marvel at this wonder of the appearing of mankind glorified by God.

Chapter 5 in Summary

1. **The church is the one, holy, catholic, and apostolic communion of God as it appears amidst each society.** This display of the power of the resurrection to bring about the reconciliation of world is the distinctive contribution of the church to the life of any nation.

2. **The church is simultaneously many people and one person.** This reconciliation of one and many is played out in the form of every Christian gathering. This head and this body face each other, and this body must be reconciled to this head.

3. **Each church has to recognize this single Christian as the gift of Christ.** We have to take each leader as the *presence* of Christ to us. Each Christian, and Christian leader, has to recognize the whole Christian people as the people Christ has given him to, and for whom he is responsible.

4. **Christ sends the apostle who is most humbling to us.** This is why leadership is always the most testing issue. The apostle is Christ unrecognized, who has to suffer our dismay and revulsion at the darkness of the cross that represents the extent of our sin and helplessness.

5. **The service of the church is to bless the society to which it is given.** It talks that society up, and enables it to pull back from self-destruction.

6. **The church that declares the limits to the authority of the worldly powers is prepared to undergo the suffering that results from this witness.** The church is able to undergo the suffering transferred to it by a society that is in denial about its own limits. To those in power and most anxious to silence it, the church always appears to be suffering and in crisis.

7. **Together with our Lord we are being made holy through undergoing a continuing passion at the hands of the world.** Christ is suffering, rejected, despised by our society; those who abuse us, defy him, and destroy themselves. Whenever their rejection turns violent, the church more truly becomes the body of Christ, increasingly able to realize and reveal that the passion of Christ is the way God is sharing his glory with the world.

8. **The eucharistic elements are miniature embodiments of Christ's passion.** This bread represents "being broken," and so indicates that the church is breaking and opening itself for the world so that the world can feed on it. This wine indicates that the church is to be poured out as a drink offering, for the world which is likely to reject it.

9. **The eucharistic bread and wine are embodiments of Christ's victory, and first installments of the reconciliation, fulfillment, and perfection of all things.** They are the unity of Christ and church in one body, and they bring that order and unity to creation. Bread and wine are embodiments of the passion and resurrection simultaneously.

10. **We are being integrated into Christ and into one another.** Christ is the whole loaf with his people. The bread displays the uniting, coming into existence, and coming together of the body of Christ. The body of Christ is incorporating us into itself. Eating this loaf is analogue to our being incorporated into this indivisible body.

11. **The proper context of the eucharist is the transformation and sanctification of mankind and creation.** They are the work-in-progress of the ongoing priesthood of Christ. This living relationship must be presented in dynamic terms, not in the static terms of substance and presence. What we say about any creature depends its future, its redemption, and its participation in the eternal life God intends for it. What is living cannot be defined by what is dead.

12. **The Holy Spirit has taken hold of us, put us in Christ's possession and is now making us present to one another.** We cannot lay hands on Christ, and cannot put ourselves out of his reach. This "presence" is not reciprocal. We are present to him, but he is not present to us. The very fact that we cannot see him, grasp and seize him is guarantee that he is the Lord, not us.

13. **The indivisible and indestructible Holy Spirit supplies us with many witnesses, saints, and gifts of holiness.** Endlessly able to divide himself, he remains indivisible.

14. **Christ has freed us from the compulsion to force one another.** We can no longer devour one another. He commands us to grasp and hold onto him with all the force of which we are capable.

15. **Mankind is the point at which creation becomes free, and at which eternity enters creation, lending immortality to mortal creatures.**

16. **Christ is the whole Christ, the head and the body.** When he is head and body, we may also become part of this body. We are the body because he makes us so and constantly sustains us as his. He makes us holy and does so in order that the world can see through us to him.

17. **The Holy Spirit keeps Christ distinct from us.** The absolute difference between the Lord's divinity and our createdness remains clear, so he is not absorbed into the church, but forever remains God, and *our* God.

18. **Christ makes us present to one another, to God, and to all creation.** Our existence and presence are fitful, based on promise and hope. God brings us into being and sets us before one another, in the hope that all will receive the approval of all.

19. **The church is the image of the future of all mankind, redeemed and glorified.** Whatever is happening to the church now is for the glory of God and the glory that God gives to us.

Endnotes

1. See https://www.churchofengland.org/prayer-and-worship/worship-texts-and-resources/common-worship/ministry/common-worship-ordination-0#nrp2-8.

2. Augustine, *Expositions of the Psalms: Vol. 2, Ps 33–50*, translation and notes by Maria Boulding, edited by John E. Rotelle (New York: New City, 2000), 85.1 (p. 220).

3. Augustine, *City of God*, translated by Henry Bettenson (Harmondsworth: Penguin Classics, 1984), 10.20 (p. 401).

4. Augustine, *Essential Sermons*, edited by Daniel Doyle, translated by Edmund Hill (Hyde Park, NY: New York City Press, 2007), *Serm.* 272 (p. 318).

5. Augustin, *Serm.* 229.

6. Augustin, *Serm.* 227.

7. Augustine, *Civ.* 10.6.

Index

Adoration, 2–3, 56, 64–65
Altar, 11, 13, 36–37, 39, 80, 117, 121
Anamnesis, 12–13
Anaphora, 39, 80, 178
Animals, animal bodies, 79, 109, 119, 122, 163, 172–73
Antiphony, 70–71
Apostle, 44, 50, 84, 134, 136–9
Ascent, ascension, 15, 24, 28, 43, 175, 177
Assembly, 18, 43, 59, 79, 85, 93, 153, 158, 174
Atonement, 40, 61–2, 115–16, 126–29
Augustine, 97, 151–52, 162–63, 165–66

Baptism, 49–51, 56, 82
Benedict, Saint (Rule of), 108
Bishop, 96, 134–40, 177
Blessing, 16, 63–66, 106–7, 127, 137, 139, 149–50
Blood, 38, 77, 80, 92, 119, 122–23, 161, 167–70
Body, 13–15, 18–19, 32, 39, 41, 44–5, 49–50, 76–80, 82–83, 99, 101, 109–10, 116–17, 119–21, 126, 140, 149, 151–53, 157–58, 161–63, 170–73, 175, 177–78
Bread (loaf), 11–14, 40–42, 79–80, 166, 168
Breaking of bread, 11, 41, 168–69
Buying & selling, 110–11

Catholic, catholicity, 50, 83, 98, 109, 134–36, 138, 140, 143

Christ, the Whole Christ, head and body, 4–5, 7–8, 38–40, 44–45, 72–73, 77–78, 84–85, 116, 126, 128–29, 152–53, 157–58
City, 89–90, 96–97, 107–8, 110–15
Communion (of saints), 3, 11, 40–41, 149 156, 162–63, 175–77
Confidence (and trust), 33, 112, 160
Congregation, 31, 62, 70, 83–85, 126, 138, 143
Consume, consumer, consumption, 41, 56, 103–4, 113, 115, 119–23, 169, 172–73
Consummation, 80–81, 177
Correction, 53, 65, 137–38
Covenant, 72, 94, 100, 102, 105, 159
Creation, 11, 13, 35–36, 63, 79–80, 105, 145–46, 167–68, 171–72, 174, 177–78
Credit, 63, 110–11
Creed, 6, 50
Cross (way of the cross), 12, 17, 23, 38, 72–73, 108, 112–14, 115–18, 126–29
Crucifixion, 13, 72, 112, 116, 128, 157
Cult, 65–66, 84, 103–4, 108–9
Cup (wine), 77, 101, 114, 121–23, 166–67, 169

Death, 12, 19, 37–38, 50–51, 69, 116, 158, 178
Debt, 121–23
Despair, 54, 104–5, 123–25
Discipline, discipleship, 57–8, 65, 83, 90–91, 99, 135, 138

Division, 126, 168, 170
Doctrine, 138, 142, 146

Easter, 45, 53, 69, 164,
Eat, eating, 41, 80, 119–21, 168–69, 171–73
Economy, 111, 113, 117, 121
Ecumenism, 84, 136
Eucharist, 11–13, 37–41, 75–79, 80–81, 162–73
Eternity, 163, 173, 175, 178–79

Faith, 6, 7, 10, 45, 58, 138, 143
Family, 94–95, 102, 169
Festivals, fasts, 53, 67, 76, 100, 121
Finance, 110–11
Food, 38, 79, 119–21, 171–72
Forgiveness, 10, 33, 35–36, 61–62, 73, 91–93, 155
Freedom, 6, 32, 79–80, 82, 99, 124, 144–45, 154–55
Future, 55, 80–83, 85, 144, 153, 156, 174, 179

Gather, gathering, 8, 18, 55–56, 79, 83, 134–35, 153–54
Glory, 2, 8, 25–7, 60, 64, 84–85, 118, 125–29
God, 4–6, 9, 25–26, 176
Gods, other gods, 25–26, 51, 56, 103, 117, 123
Gospel, 27–29, 57, 61, 101–2, 106–7, 114
Government, 91–92, 94–96, 150

History, 55, 85, 93, 148, 176,
Holy Spirit, 7–8, 32, 45, 70, 77–78, 84, 152
Holy, holiness, 3, 8, 41–2, 55
Hope, 102, 104, 165, 179
Humanity, 44, 80, 82, 156, 175
Hymns, songs, 31, 62, 68–69

Image (icon), 18, 85, 128, 154, 179
Intercessions, 9, 33–34, 78–79, 137–38

Judge, judgment, 5, 33, 36, 58–61, 89, 93–97, 112–14, 122–24, 127

Lament, 16, 91, 113, 115–17
Law, 95
Leader, 135
Learning, 99, 164
Life, 11, 18–19, 50–51, 63, 66, 76–77, 81
Liturgy, 18, 61, 97, 103–4, 153–55
Lord's Supper (Last Supper), 11–14, 38
Love, 3, 32, 56, 64–65, 82, 99, 102–3, 104–5, 109–10, 116, 151, 155, 159

Mankind, 44, 61–62, 65, 72–73, 79–80, 103, 112, 115–17, 128–29, 145–49
Man and woman, 56, 94, 100, 102
Market, market place, 65, 108–12
Marks of the Church, 50
Marriage, 94, 99–102
Materiality, 14, 79, 119–21, 167, 174, 177–78
Mission, 15, 57, 123
Mystery, 62, 81, 145–46, 150, 176

Narrative, 5–6, 58–62, 68–70, 177

Offering, 11, 39, 80, 136, 162, 166, 178
Ordain, ordination, 98–99, 142

Palm Sunday, 24, 53
Passion, 12–3, 37–38, 102, 118, 128–29, 155–60
Passover, 11, 37–38, 61, 108, 166
Persecution, 160–61
Prayer, 8–11, 33–34, 71, 162
Preaching. *See* Sermon
Priest, priesthood, 40–41, 74, 80, 83, 135, 140, 165
Procession, 23–24, 43, 51–52, 54–55, 89, 93, 109–10, 113, 115, 160
Psalm, 31
Public square, 96–97, 105–8

Recognition, 2, 63–65, 75, 176

Index

Reconciliation, 36, 74, 80, 84, 91–92, 102, 136, 178
Redemption, 42, 118, 121
Remembering, remembrance, 12
Repentance, 34–36, 73, 112–14
Responsibility, 100–102, 137, 150
Resurrection, 42, 45, 55, 70, 81–82, 85, 153, 156

Sacraments, 41, 76–77, 165
Sacrifice, 103, 112, 117–18, 151–52, 162–67
Saints, 43, 55, 85, 118, 154, 160–61, 166–67, 169
Salvation, 19, 104, 115–16, 126–29, 158–9
Sanctification, 42, 90, 163–65, 177
Scripture, 4–6, 27–29, 31, 58–59, 140–42
Secular, secularity, secularisation, 96–97, 104–6, 141, 144, 154–55
Sermon, 5–6, 28, 31, 58–59
Service, 7–8, 11, 15–16, 30, 43, 57, 60, 112, 115

Sin, 19, 34–37, 38, 42, 73–75, 101–2, 141–42, 160
Singing, 6–7, 17, 30–32, 53, 62–63, 67–71, 91
Soul, 99
Speech, 17, 32, 64
State, 150

Teaching, 20 143, 147–48
Testament (Old, New), 4–5, 27, 29, 31, 44, 58, 61
Thanks, thanksgiving, 3, 6–7, 11–12, 30–31, 66, 106–7, 167
Tradition, 50, 62, 99, 101, 138

University, 145–48

Versification (rhyme, rhythm), 68–69

Water, 51–52, 141
Witness, witnesses, 26, 31, 43, 53–54, 57, 95, 98, 118, 123, 141

www.ingramcontent.com/pod-product-compliance
Lightning Source LLC
Chambersburg PA
CBHW031430150426
43191CB00006B/465